Fishing with Kids
A Parent's Guide

John Paxton

ISBN: 978-1-7344672-0-8 (paper edition)
ISBN: 978-1-7344672-1-5 (e-book edition)

Published by John Paxton
Photographs and cover by the author.

www.fishingfather.com

DEDICATION

This book is dedicated to Tristan and Amber.

CONTENTS

ACKNOWLEDGMENTS

This book would not have been possible but for the love and attention a great number of adults gave to me as I was a young child learning to fish along the shores of Lake Champlain. I owe this book to my father, John, my Uncle Steve, and their good friends George and Pat. Their patience, enthusiasm, knowledge, and willingness to hand off their rod, regardless of how big a fish was on the end of it, all contributed to make fishing a lifelong passion that I now share with my kids.

I'd also like to thank all the authors who have come before me and taught me much of what I know. Special credit is owed to the staff at *In-Fishermen* who produced a series of books that I absolutely cherished as a child. Their *Northern Pike Secrets: An In-Fisherman Handbook of Strategies* was one of the first books I ever wore out, though it wouldn't be the last. I highly recommend that you pick it up.

My wife, Crystal deserves considerable thanks for allowing me considerable leeway over the years to pursue this passion (including pretending she didn't know darn well I was headed north to buy a boat) and for the wonderful children she gave me.

Finally, my two children, Tristan and Amber, naturally deserve the lion's share of credit. If it wasn't for the way their eyes light up when I hand them a fishing pole, I would have never been inspired to write this book.

It is my hope that this book as well as my blog www.fishingfather.com will help parents everywhere spark joy and wonder in their children's eyes as they share the pastime of fishing with a new generation.

1 – A LIFE WORTH LIVING

The author fishing with his father.

There are only two things worth having in life: family and fishing lures. Yes, you might think food or shelter rank as well, but if you have a loving family by your side and they all know how to fish, food's taken care of, and you can always sell your leftovers for a place to hang your hat.

I had my priorities straightened from a very young age by my father. He had bought an old run-down lake house on Lake Champlain when I was three, and my earliest memories of him were seeing him pack up his suitcase to head north each weekend to fix it up. It always made me cry to see him go, and I'd try to hide in his suitcase so I could trick him into taking me.

I never did manage to fool him, and so it went every weekend for what seemed like years: Dad would come home from work, pack up a suitcase, and head off to work on the house. I would cry and put up a big fuss and try to convince him to take me, but he'd always decline. It got to such a point where I stopped trying to hide in the suitcase, and all but gave up.

My luck changed one glorious day in 1991. He picked me up in one arm, grabbed my suitcase in another, and carried me towards his car. He said we were headed up to Crown Point to meet up with his best friend, a man I always knew as "Uncle Steve." We traveled the 220 miles north listening to marginally inappropriate Jimmy Buffet and Marty Robbins songs while he told me amazing stories of giant northern pike and more bass than I could count (which, being six-years-old, might have meant all of 10 or 20).

The drive is only supposed to take about four hours, but with little kids it's usually seven, so it was evening already by the time we got there—too late to fish that night, but still early enough to hear my uncle's fishing stories from the day. Boy, did he ever fill my head. He talked about far-off bays he'd never visited and all the fish they held.

I remember seeing Dad and Steve study their maps and charts as Uncle Steve pointed out exactly where Dad should take me – despite what you've heard about "lying fishermen," there are no secret spots when you're trying to put your best friend's kid on fish. Uncle Steve hooked Dad up with the right place and the right tackle and now all we needed to do was figure out a way to get me to fall asleep, so I'd be fresh for the next day.

Given how excited I was, I wouldn't have blamed him if he resorted to cough medicine, but I'm pretty sure he was more patient than that and after a few vexing few hours, I finally managed to close my eyes.

The next morning was one for the ages. Our house is on the New York side of the lake, so I was treated to a brilliant sunrise with the gentle, rolling farmlands of Vermont in the background. It's the promise of this sight that gets me through each winter and warms my soul the first time I see it each year. It's hard to look at something as beautiful as that and not whisper a quiet "thank you" to God, so that's what I did on that morning and every time I've seen it since.

We hopped in Dad's boat, which at that time was still new and started easily with a gentle purr and little smoke. Even though the three seats were in a line from bow to stern, I sat down on the floor between some dried-up worm guts and Dad as he gently worked the throttle and eased us off the dock.

The historian in me has spent a fair amount of time trying to determine exactly where we went. I'd love to know exactly where I became a fisherman for life, but Dad can't remember, and I can't quite place it no matter how many bays I visit. All I know is it was some reed-filled bay south of Crown Point and far, far away. Perhaps it was that old bay north of the paper mill, or maybe it was down near the fort. It felt like it took us forever to reach it, but once we arrived it was clear why my uncle had sent us.

Despite the distance, it was still early, and a mist still hung over the calm, smooth water. Every now and then, a fish broke the surface, just to remind you the water wasn't glass. There were tall, light-tan reeds everywhere in that bay. While most of these formed a wall, there were gaps in it – little coves and alleyways filled with dark, clear water and all the fishy expectations that a child's head could fit.

I picked up my rod and carefully selected the perfect lure for it – a golden yellow spinnerbait with big, painted red eyes with a black pupil. Dad helped me rig it as he didn't want me to get hurt. He showed me how to unclasp a snap swivel and thread it through the circle on the spinnerbait's bent wire arm.

He put his hand on my shoulder and leaned in, whispering in my ear, "Right there, John – cast right in that pocket between the reeds!" My first effort sailed well to the left, deep in the reed wall – Dad had to grab the rod quickly and give it a few short tugs while reeling fast to make sure it came out alright without spoiling the nearby pool.

He handed it to me again, and patiently helped me take the line on my forefinger and flip the bail, while telling me to give it another go. I carefully brought it backwards and then snapped it forward with all my might, but I let go of the line too early, so the lure landed somewhere behind us with a splash!

I'm sure Dad rolled his eyes a bit, but we stuck with it and on the third time I finally nailed it! The spinnerbait flew in a golden flash, straight and true and landed right in the back of that black, clear pocket. I started reeling immediately, just as Dad told me, and before it broke free from this little cove, my rod bent over double – fish on!

I don't remember what that first fish was. Maybe it was a pickerel, or perhaps a largemouth bass. It matters not. All that I know is that it was the first time I felt that jolt up my arm as I became connected to another creature by a short stretch of monofilament. I could feel its energy, and it could feel mine. We were locked in a battle that only one could win, and while I had every intention of throwing the fish back, who could blame it for thinking we were playing for keeps? The fish fought well, and the experience was unlike anything I'd known before. It was one of which I'd never tire.

When it was my turn to be "Dad" a quarter century later, I knew I had to share this feeling with my son.

Becoming a Fishing Father

It was many casts before I met my son. A lifetime's worth, by some accounts, as fishing was a main pastime of our family and had been for decades at least, and maybe longer. Each father taught his sons what he knew, and each son eventually taught their dad even more. The wives and sisters often came along and usually out fished the boys, a tradition my own wife maintains.

Back then it was just Dad and the three of us. While he worked hard, partied harder, and wasn't always around, he would never pass up a chance to go fishing with his kids.

His favorite place to take us was Lake Champlain. It was always an ordeal driving up, with the kids bickering over this and that and crying in-between. It didn't get any easier on Dad when we finally pulled down the driveway, as he would have to unload the car while we all went careening towards the lake, tripping over each other and skinning knees and crying for his help. It's no wonder he used to curse so much, and a miracle he never drank.

He would somehow fit all three of us on that little boat of his. There wasn't even a seat for everyone, so one or the other used the floor. We'd all turn our caps backwards as the boat gained speed and headed off towards Vermont, lest the wind steal our hat and send it towards the drink.

Dad's favorite means of fishing with all of us in tow was just to drift along the shoreline twitching marabou jigs and green, straight-tailed grubs, seeking panfish, smallmouth, and whatever else would bite. It was easy enough, unless the wind got out of hand, and allowed him to spend his time on the vexing tasks of untangling lines and removing fish from lures and arms from hooks. It seemed that as soon as he had untangled one line, another was handed to him. For the grief we gave him, it's remarkable he was as composed as he was.

When the three of us had enough, or dad needed stitches, we'd head back in to shore. Sometimes he'd have chores to do and would set us up with some stout rods rigged with minnows or cut bait, telling us to sit on the dock, watch out for each other, and hold on. We'd sit there and pass the time singing songs or pretending we saw the local lake monster, Champ. Eventually, one of our rods would twitch, then double over, and we'd swear we hooked him. A large channel cat or bowfin can twist a young imagination quick on that lake.

We eventually grew old enough that we could all cast on our own. Dad taught us how to speed spinnerbaits over sunken weeds or hop jigs along a rocky point. He'd coach us to "keep [our] rod tip high!" and "reel, reel, reel!" as we'd burn timber king weedless spoons across a grass flat or fight a charging pike. We watched as he adjusted our drift down the shore or motored up to a familiar point or bay. We would listen intently as he would explain what crankbaits he had used in this tournament or that and under what conditions, and when bites were scarce and nothing else was working, we'd watch expectantly as he threaded on the little tan one with the brown, vertical stripes – "the cheating lure," as he called it.

Sometimes, we would start our day with a trip to the local bait shop to talk shop with Dad's friends, George and Pat. Other times, if we were lucky, we'd end the day there with a giant fish for releasing in the swamp out back. On occasion, if Dad was really pressed for time, he'd ask George and Pat to take us out themselves, and then we'd really light them up. Those two were great at vertical jigging for numbers of panfish and bass of good size and taught me much about how to keep fishing fun for kids.

As with many teens, when I grew older, Dad and I grew apart. Adolescence is not the time most children spend with their parents, but despite this we'd still get together from time to time to go fishing. Looking back, I wish we'd gone much more as it would have kept me out of trouble. I certainly would have made better decisions with how to spend my money, effort, and time. It's hard to spend any of those on questionable teenage plots when you've already spent them on spinnerbaits. Kids get in a lot less trouble when they have expensive hobbies.

I kept that thought in mind years later when I had my own son, and even a bit earlier, when he was but a twinkle in my eye. It's no exaggeration to say that – at least since getting married – every book I've read on fishing, every new technique I've tried, and every time I took someone else's children onto my boat for a few hours has been, at least to some extent, with the aim of learning something new I could one day teach children of my own.

By the time my son was born, I had assembled an arsenal of tackle, decades of experience, and a few hard lessons from taking out other people's kids. I couldn't wait to get him out on the water and brought him to see Lake Champlain for the first time when he was only a few months old. As with most newborns, he spent the time oblivious and squinting from the sun, but the following spring, he was ready and engaged.

Being just less than a year old the following Memorial Day, he wasn't doing any casting or even any reeling, just playing with his mother in the boat and scurrying up whenever I pulled in a new fish. He showed no fear of them and seemed to think they were the coolest thing. He wanted to touch them, which I let him do with wet hands. As he learned to speak over that summer, he started talking about fish. He called blue gill "boogala" and chain pickerel "Boo boo fish," because I wouldn't let him hold them.

I did all I could to keep the momentum through the winter, as we practiced reeling in our living room. I took the hooks off a plug and would cast towards the corner. Then, I'd hand him the rod and say "reel, reel, reel!" He would want to try casting too, but to spare the television and the dog, I managed to resist the urge to let him try.

That was a long winter for us, but as soon as the ice cleared, I brought him out, hooked a largemouth bass, and handed him the rod to reel it in. His eyes lit up, he was giggling non-stop, and jumping in place while he reeled it in. I understood what my own dad must have felt like all those casts ago.

The author fishing with his son.

If you've bought this book, it's a solid bet that you're interested in making some of these memories of your own. I'm confident that each one of you can achieve this, but there are a few steps that will help you get there.

Step 1: Adjust Your Attitude

As you can tell, I had some great memories fishing with my dad and I'm making even more now fishing with my kids. I want the same for you, and I'm going to do my best throughout this book to help you get there, but it's all going to be for naught if you approach this with the wrong attitude.

It's easy to get caught up in visions of perfect sunrises, willing fish, and laughing children. You will, at times, live that dream, but other times you won't! Fishing can very challenging. While each individual step isn't all that complicated, putting it all together can be perplexing and there is so much that can go wrong. Even when fishing alone, you'll find yourself retrieving hooks from trees, untangling nests of fishing line, retying lures, and other issues. Kids make these issues a thousand times worse, and you need to be prepared for that.

Your attitude is going to be the deciding factor in whether your kids have a good time. Remember, they are new to this and have no expectations except whatever ones you set. The only thing that really matters to them is that they get to spend time with you. If every tangle or other mishap brings out your inner ogre, they're going to be too scared to keep trying, and they're going to need to do a *ton* of trying before they start succeeding in a sport like fishing.

With all that in mind, it's time for some basic accountability up front, well before you get your kids anywhere near the shoreline. If you're an even-keeled kind of person, my hat's off to you. If not, what causes you to become agitated? Will a lack of sleep do you in? Will hunger? What about the sun in your eyes or feeling too hot or cold? Do you get stressed out when you're interrupted while trying to work through something precise? Can you deal with making a mistake? How do you handle that?

Knowing what sets you off is half the battle, because you can take the necessary steps to mitigate your chance of having a bad day. Here are some of the more common reasons I've seen people get frustrated while on the water, and some tips for how to prepare for them ahead of time, or deal with them as they occur:

- Lack of sleep: It can be very challenging to fall asleep the night before a fishing trip. There is much to prepare, and you're doing this all with a growing excitement. Even so, if you're the sort of person who gets flustered when tired, you need to do your best to get a good night's sleep. Packing up your gear and tackle earlier in the week is a great start. Then you only need to make the kids' lunches the night before and can get some sleep.

- Hunger: I will admit that I get hangry. I know this about myself and realize that if I don't get a good breakfast in me and have plenty of snacks, I'm not going to be at my best out there. It's simple enough to fix, at least as snacks go (just make sure they're filling enough), but I'm as prone as the next fisherman to be too excited in the morning to want to spend much time or effort making an elaborate breakfast. Here too you can prepare the night before. Some breakfast foods, like sausage or kielbasa, do very well in the fridge overnight. Anything you can prepare the night before and just reheat is going to help you the morning of your fishing trip.

- Temperature: You will never be colder, or sweat more, than when you're on a boat. Being in the middle of the lake, often unprotected from the elements, can be terrible if you don't have the proper clothing. Remember that you can always remove layers as needed, but you can't add on anything if you don't have it. Overdress, and remember to zip up your rain jacket.

- Interruptions: Sorry to break it to you, but when you're fishing with kids, you're going from one interruption to the next. These are going to come at inopportune times, such as when you're in the middle of tying a knot. You can't do much about the interruptions, but you can at least try to make individual tasks less daunting, so interruptions are less damaging. For example, you could tie up a few rigs before you head out and just use a snap swivel and barrel swivel to connect them, as discussed in Chapter 5. The little fish that your kids are after won't mind and having stuff ready to go will save you time.

- Mistakes: You're going to make plenty of mistakes out there, up to and including losing that giant fish that your kid hooked because you either hit it with the net, or perhaps didn't land it fast enough. You could be tempted to let your frustration with yourself out after such a disaster, but your five-year-old isn't going to realize that you're mad at yourself; they're going to think you're mad at them. They're going to think they messed up, when they didn't, which can rapidly sour their day. Unfortunately, you can't do much to prepare for this ahead of time. Raising your comfort level with fishing in general before you try to take your kids out for the first time would help, but you're still going to mess up often – even the pros do. The only thing you can do when something bad happens is laugh at yourself, throw your hands up in the air, and say "woops!" Get your kids doing it too and then it doesn't even matter if they land the fish (a word of warning: you can be too successful at this strategy. You'll know you went overboard when you find them almost disappointed when you manage to land one).

If there is any advantage to these issues, it's that all of these problems can trigger your kids as easily as you, so being prepared for these things to happen to you will often also make you more prepared for it to happen to them. Any parent who has seen their child about to cry can tell you that catching them right before a meltdown is far easier than trying to walk them away from the ledge after a crying fit has begun.

Step 2: Set Expectations

It's vitally important to set expectations for your kids when planning a fishing trip. They ought to know about how long it's going to take to get to the fishing spot, what your plan is once you get there, and how the fish might not bite right away. You're much better off presenting this as a fun puzzle to figure out rather than a guaranteed success. If a kid thinks they're going off to try and figure out what the fish want like some sort of detective, they'll have much more patience when it takes a few different presentations or fishing spots to do just that.

It's always better to under promise and over deliver on a fishing trip. "Let's go hang out at the lake and try and see if we can catch any fish" is better than "let's go catch some giant fish and show mommy!" I'm going to do everything I can in this book to help you put your little ones on fish, but success if not guaranteed out there and even the most prepared get skunked occasionally. If your kids are planning on catching fish, that can be a problem. I've made this mistake before and heard the, "But daddy, *you didn't let me* catch any fish" when it was time to go home. It's not a good look and one you want to avoid!

It's just as important to set your own expectations. Look, we've all seen the videos on YouTube of the little kids stomping about and giggling as they reel in giant fish, and every parent out there wants to have that moment. You will have yours, but don't be disappointed if it doesn't happen immediately. These things take time.

It's much more likely that your first few attempts will be bumbling and awkward, with plenty of tangles, several lures lost in the trees, and nary a fish. This can either be a challenging experience or can be a comedy of errors filled with plenty of laughs. It all depends on how you prepare for it and where you set your expectations.

Another important consideration is that your children just might not be into fishing. That's OK. If this isn't for them, it isn't for them. That doesn't mean they won't like boating, or hiking, or birdwatching, or exploring and playing with frogs and newts and all the interesting bugs that might be near your local pond. Just because they don't want to cast out a lure doesn't mean that they can't be part of the fun – there are plenty of great memories to be made with your kids on your next vacation, regardless of their interest level in fishing.

Step 3: Read, Read, Read

Angling is a life-long pursuit with a large learning curve, so anglers tend to be voracious readers. There are library's worth of books out there in the world that can help you enhance your skillset and further your success. I encourage you to seek these out and read them with your kids.

Reading about fishing with your kids helps prepare for the next trip and enhances their ability to retain knowledge and learn. It's a hoot to hear a young kid speak up and explain that you need to get closer to the reeds so you can cast "palalel" (parallel) to them and have a better chance of drawing a strike.

The more time you spend studying fishing books with your kids, the more tricks you and they will learn to help you through tough situations. It's not always going to be easy out there, but if you've read about similar circumstances, you can adjust. This also has the added benefit of helping to set both of your expectations. Even a four-year-old can look up at clear, bluebird skies, and realize that fishing won't be as great as if there was substantial cloud cover, if he remembers seeing that in a book.

Reading fishing books with your kids allows them to learn more about this sport, enhances their own reading skills, and helps spark a passion for learning that could last a lifetime. Why wouldn't you do this?

Step 4: Follow the Maxim of "Quantity Over Quality"

Always seek easily accessible fish first, with the aim of catching as many as possible. Larger fish inhabit the same general locations and will come naturally, providing a fun "bonus" while chasing panfish.

Kids just want to catch fish, period. They tend to have smaller attention spans and aren't going to tolerate long periods without any action. When given the choice, my son much prefers to fish at a local pond filled with stunted bluegill than to try his luck at a slower reservoir known for some larger fish. His ideal trip is one where he is catching something every cast (even if it isn't much bigger than a minnow). In fact, a lot of the time he wants to leave the rods at home to go catch minnows with a net!

I've ignored this maxim before and will tell you with all sincerity, do so at your peril. Any time I've gone for larger fish first, I've quickly had to backpedal and go find a school of bluegill to fill up the livewell and save the day. While it's true that you're more likely to catch larger species early in the day, you run the risk of losing your kids quickly and ruining any chance that they'll develop a passion for this sport. Wait until you have some smaller fish in the livewell for them to talk to before you switch over to larger quarry. It will make for a far better experience.

Step 5: If Something is Within Your Control, Control It

There are many things that can go wrong while you are fishing that are totally beyond your control, but there are also plenty of preventable mishaps. I would strongly urge you to do your best to control what you can.

Wear your kill switch. Have enough gas. Pack enough food and water. Make sure your knots are tied well, and that your equipment isn't damaged. Let people know where you are fishing, and when you'll return. Zip up your rain gear. Control what you can and be prepared to react effectively to what you can't.

Following this, or any of the other steps won't guarantee success, but they will certainly up the odds that you have a decent trip with some fun memories for you and your children.

2 – WHY FISHING?

If you're reading this book, you're contemplating trying to do something hard: teach a small child how to do something that requires patience. It might not be easy, but as the last chapter mentioned, it's a life worth living. Even so, sometimes I find that it is easier to brace for a difficult task if you have a great understanding of why you should bother. This chapter is going to go into some detail about a few benefits of taking your kids fishing, some of which aren't obvious.

Fishing Makes Trips to the Doctor's Easier

Yes, you read that right, folks. I have legitimately used my son's fishing experiences to help him get through a trip to the doctor's office. Before I thought of this, heading off to get a shot was a horrible experience filled with tears, begging, and fits, to say nothing of what my son would do. How did fishing change all of this, you ask? Three words: bluegill dorsal spines.

You see, my son insists on handling all his own fish and bringing them over to the livewell. With smaller fish, this means that he is routinely poked and jabbed by their dorsal spines and fins, which can feel like the prick of a shot. He just never notices this, or at least never minds it, because he's having fun and wants to handle fish "just like Daddy." I know he notices it, because he'll often say "ow," but he doesn't seem to care.

Once I made the connection, I started talking to him about bluegill and how he gets pricked frequently. Once he acknowledged that a fish spine isn't a big deal, he found that neither is getting a quick shot at the doctor's office. In fact, getting a shot at the doctor's might even be better, because it's followed by ice cream.

Fishing toughened my son up a little bit to deal with one of the scarier situations a young child will face. I wish my parents thought of this when I was his age!

A Boat is a Great Place to Potty Train Your Kids

What better place on earth is there to train your kids to use a potty than a boat? With all the blood, fish urine, worm guts, scent, and other nasties you'll drop in it on any given trip, it's not like a near-miss by your kids will make much difference, and all you have to do is hose it off later. Our boat has a vinyl floor which only makes the cleaning process even easier.

Think about it: you don't need to chase them around, there's no chance they'll ruin your couch or something else that's hard to clean, and if your kids like fishing, you'll probably be out long enough for them to "go" a few times and learn the process. Finally, they're in the middle of something they want to get back to, so they have an incentive to finish up.

Kids Love Water

Every parent knows that children love water and can't get enough of it. Fishing puts them right next to said water. Fishing is also much more entertaining for the parent than watching their children smack their hands into a splash table, and certainly less horrifying than finding them on the couch with a Tupperware "lake."

Fishing is the Antithesis of Screen Time

The more time your kids are on the water, the less time they're in front of a screen. Get your kids hooked on fishing early so you'll always have this in your back pocket to get them to go outside. Once they get hooked on this great sport, they will want to do little less.

This is because fishing keeps them engaged. Fishing is a big production and one they can be very involved in. There's all the gear to assemble and talk about, all the different species they might catch to dream of, and all the adventure of trudging through the woods to the next fishing spot or driving the boat. The television can't compete.

That's not to say the screens don't come in handy while you're fishing—I'll admit to handing my son my phone for a couple of minutes while I deal with a particularly bad tangle—but it's amazing how quickly he'll hand it back as soon as the rod is ready for more action. There are few things on earth that will pull him away from the bright lights of his favorite vlogger quicker than a fish tugging on the line.

When they ARE on Screens, It Could be "Educational"

Fishing ignited such a passion in me that even when I was in front of a screen, I was often watching a fishing program, or playing a fishing video game, like the "Black Bass" series for the Super Nintendo. I don't see either as a bad thing (there are certainly worse video games a kid could play these days).

There are many fine fishing documentaries available that will teach your children about the rhythm of nature, the seasons, and the scientific method. Fishing success is greatly enhanced by an understanding of science, and plenty of journalists have understood that since at least the 1970s. As a result, there is much knowledge out there ready to be gained.

Your kids will learn about biology, weather, the way that lakes form and age, as well as niche topics like hybridization and even just how wind and waves work. They'll likely learn a thing or two about motors and engines, about gears and their ratios, and a host of other interesting topics with applications beyond the waters.

It's never a bad thing to inspire someone to learn more about the world, and fishing is a great way to do that.

Fishing Helps Kids Learn to Listen

It sometimes feels as though the only interaction I have with my son on certain days is to repeatedly ask him, "Are you listening?" Let's face it – most of the time he isn't. He's your typical four-year-old having a million exciting adventures in his head. He has no time to hear someone tell him to eat his peas.

About the only time I can consistently count on him listening is when he has a fish on the line. I know that's counter intuitive as you'd think that pairing a small child with a live fish thrashing at the end of a hook wouldn't help them listen, but it's true. He's lost enough fish already that he doesn't want to lose more, so he is very eager to listen to my coaching when I offer it, and more importantly, apply that coaching in the future.

For example, my son knows to stop reeling frantically when he hears the "ziiiip" of line being pulled through the drag. He also does a great job of holding his rod up high, so the fish won't get any slack in the line.

He does these things because he's in the zone and really wants to land that fish. He opens to guidance, suggestions, and coaching and willing to hear what I have to say. This has worked out well for him as he has landed some fish that I don't think I would have at his age. Success with fishing breeds further success on land.

When I remember to, I can get this to extend beyond fishing. Sometimes, when I'm having a hard time getting him to focus, I grab his attention and remind him about a large fish he caught because he listened. I remind him that it's important to listen, because I'm trying to tell him something that will help him. By doing this, I'm breaking down the situation he doesn't understand (for example, why he can't break away from me in a parking lot) into one that he does (why he needs to let a fish run when it's pulling drag).

There's a method to the madness of all the fables and fairy tales we read to our kids, and the point of reading them is usually so that we can refer back to a lesson that a character learned at one point, to help our children get through life. Fishing can do that too.

Fishing Teaches Kids Strategy

The ability to think strategically is a tremendous advantage to all who possess it, and fishing is a great way to get kids to start learning some simple lessons in strategy.

Each time you go to the lake, you will have some sort of plan in mind as to where you'll start casting and what lures you'll start using. You'll likely put this plan together by trying to think of where the fish are going to be hanging around given the time of year. Whether you came up with it by scouring maps and fishing reports the night before or just by dreaming over your coffee, you've come up with a strategy.

Why not involve your children in this process?

Bring them over to the map the night before and let them know where you're thinking about fishing and why. Explain to them what you're looking for – do you suspect the fish will be at a certain depth? In certain cover? Why? Talk it through with them so they can see that you are approaching fishing thoughtfully and strategically. You'll find they soon emulate you and bring some ideas of their own.

Once they start speaking up, let them have a shot at picking the strategy for a day – you never know; they might do better than you! You'd be surprised at just how quickly kids can take to this, and if they're completely hooked on the sport and reading about it on their own, chances are they've stumbled across some information that you've missed.

Fishing Teaches Kids to Deal with Change

Anyone who has been in corporate America for any length of time knows and dreads the term, "Change Management." It is so pervasive that it stands to reason it is one of the critical skills we can teach our children. Change will be constant throughout their lives and will create chaos unless they know how to take a deep breath and muddle through.

Fishing is great for teaching kids about change because it's everywhere in the sport. The successful fisherman knows when to switch things up when a certain plan isn't working.

The seasons are the most glaring example of change and offer a good way to talk to children about the seasonal patterns of fish, where you can expect to find them during the year, and how active they might be.

With the seasons come changes in the local flora and hiding spots for fish. One Lake Champlain bay I favor couldn't be a better example. Early in the spring, most of the weeds are still budding on the bottom and haven't reached the surface. It is possible to pull jerkbaits and crankbaits through with very little snagging, and the bay often holds large northern pike as its waters are still cool. Just a few weeks later, that same bay is filled with weeds and barren of pike as the warm waters entice plenty of pickerel and bass but push off the larger predator. I often fish there with my son the first week of May, Memorial Day, and then again on the 4th of July. The relatively short time between each trip allows him to remember what we faced just a short while ago and marvel at how quickly it changed.

As transformative as just a few weeks makes, change can be much more rapid in fishing. The tides are a good example as the rock or jetty that you caught so many fish on earlier might soon be consumed by the sea, forcing you to try something different. Likewise, just a shift in the wind often either turns on a hectic bite or completely shuts one down.

Even small things, like the process of losing a trusted fishing lure to a snag brings about change. It's not a fun feeling to be forced to move from one technique that was catching fish in droves to something else that's unproven for the day, but sometimes that's exactly what you need to do.

Fishing Teaches Problem Solving Skills

Problems arise frequently while fishing. Having your kids observe you while you solve a few (and then having them solve a few on their own) teaches kids to work through a tough situation and come up with a solution. Just try not to approach said problems with too many curse words or prepare to teach your kids those as well!

Rather than waiting for a problem to come to you, a better place to teach problem solving might be with wacky-rigged worms. If you've ever used them, you know that just rigging them right on a hook is an expensive proposition as they tend to tear off the hook easily and are lost. Go ahead – show your kids how easily this happens – there's the problem, now how to solve it?

Well, you may have heard of sliding o-rings up the middle of the worm and then attaching your hook to the ring instead, as it tends to extend the use you'll get out of the bait. This solves a problem and teaches your kids to start looking for solutions instead of just complaining or giving up.

I'll discuss o-rings a bit more in Chapter 5 and explain an interesting way to easily rig them with a tool you already own.

Fishing Lets Kids Provide for Others

My children are still young, so I know this is probably fleeting, but now at least, they're both very interested in being helpful. My son enjoys vacuuming, because he gets to be "part of the team" and even my daughter enjoys throwing things away in the garbage if you ask her to. While I harbor no illusions that this will continue for boring old chores, people need a purpose in life, and kids are no different. Fishing can help give them one to latch on to when they're too young to know of much else.

While I would encourage everyone to practice a "selective harvest" (described below), fishing is a great way to put food on the table, and one of the few ways that a young child can contribute to the production and livelihood of the family.

If your family relies on nature for meat, letting your children take part in gathering it will make them feel relevant, important, and esteemed. Most kids want to pull their weight. Fishing is a great way for them to do that.

Fishing Teaches A Greater Respect for Nature

I mentioned selective harvest above. It's not a term I came up with (I believe the credit belongs to the staff of *In-Fishermen*), but it's an idea worth spreading. The theory is that both catch & take as well as catch & release both miss the mark in different ways.

If one were to eat every fish they caught, they would soon find themselves with no fish left to catch. Yet at the same time, throwing back every fish can lead to overpopulation and stunted growth, especially in smaller ponds.

The idea behind selective harvest is that you want to release the truly large and magnificent fish as they are the ones genetically predisposed to have babies that will also grow to massive proportion. Instead, you should focus on keeping and eating smaller fish (where legal) who are more abundant (and usually taste better too).

Practicing this and teaching it to your kids will tend to get them thinking about the natural order of things and how they can negatively influence nature if they aren't careful.

Fishing will teach your kids about conservation in other ways. For example, you'd do well to take a little bag out for garbage whenever you're taking your kids fishing. First, kids create a massive amount of garbage all on their own, seemingly out of thin air. More importantly, when your child observes you going through the effort to lean over and pick some trash up, they are more likely to appreciate why we shouldn't litter and become better stewards for the planet.

Likewise, police up your fishing line. Don't let it stay stuck in the tree, or just toss it on the ground. Explain to your children how birds and other animals can become trapped or ensnared by the line and encourage your children to always pick up after themselves.

If you explain why you're taking the time to clean up after others, it will be a good start for your budding conservationists.

Fishing Teaches Self-Reliance and Resiliency

Often, when things go wrong out on the water you must fix them yourself. Perhaps you have an issue with a battery connection, or maybe all your tackle gets tangled up. No one is going to fix these issues for you, but your kids will certainly watch with a keen eye while you attempt a remedy.

I remember I was once out fishing some miles from home, having a grand old time and absolutely slaying some pickerel when I looked back and noticed my boat was sinking! I didn't know it at the time, but the livewell intake had broken clean off the boat and was flooding the bilge.

This was an interesting dilemma, to say the least. I pointed my trolling motor in the direction of home and started frantically bailing (this old boat didn't have a bilge pump, naturally). Anyway, I managed to bail it enough to where I thought I could use the outboard. I got home, retrieved the boat and saw the problem.

This was, of course, right at the start of my vacation and I thought it was all over. My boat had a giant hole in it, after all! Luckily, my friend introduced me to the amazing curative powers of epoxy and after finding an appropriate plug we were able to get everything nice and dry and keep on fishing.

Telling your kids little stories like that (or living them out right next to each other) can make a big difference in how self-reliant they grow to be.

Self-reliance and resiliency go hand in hand. The more self-reliant one is, the more resilient they tend to become, as they're confident in their abilities to weather the storm. Even so, fishing teaches resiliency in a less heartwarming fashion – things flat out go wrong that can't be undone.

Not all fish that are hooked will be landed, and having your child go through this minor disappointment repeatedly will begin to teach them resilience and how to move on from setbacks without throwing a temper tantrum. This will only work, however, if the adult they're fishing with is a good role model and just lets it go with a smile.

If a fish breaks off the line, it's very tempting to let your frustration get the best of you and start complaining or groaning. Avoid this temptation and instead just focus on how much fun it was to fight the fish. "Gosh that sure was a big one! Let's see if we can catch him again!" Often, fish school and another large one is just a few casts away!

Fishing Rewards Hard Work While Delaying Gratification

I'm on the parental soap box at this point and there's no stepping off. Two more virtues every kid needs to learn are the rewards of hard work and how to delay gratification. Fishing teaches both.

Sometimes you must really work for a bite. While this isn't a great situation to be in with toddlers (you *really* want to make things as easy as possible for them), older kids can start to develop a good work ethic by fishing.

An angler often carefully prepares their gear well into the night and then rises before the sun to drive to the lake, launch the boat, and head out fishing. Hundreds if not thousands of casts may be made throughout the day, and dozens if not more knots will be retied. They may or may not hook a fish during this process, but if they do, they'll need to be skillfully played and landed. When the day is up, the boat needs to be retrieved, drained, and dried. Then everything needs to be packed up for the night. It can often be a 14-hour "workday."

Just in case it isn't obvious, you should NOT take your kids out for that long, but if they love fishing, they might start talking about becoming a professional angler. That's a wonderful opportunity to talk about how hard the pros work and how much they sacrifice. For the most part, professional fishermen are good role models for your kids. Take advantage of that and use it to get your kids to start cleaning their room!

This whole process will also teach kids about delayed gratification. Fishing is a sport where delayed gratification is almost constantly involved. You do certain tasks in the hopes of being rewarded in the future. This is an important task for children to learn or else they will turn into college grads wondering why they can't immediately land a six-figure job.

Granted, with small kids, you'll want to do your best to make sure that the delayed gratification is as brief as possible (I've found about five seconds enough for a two-year-old), so there is a balance here. Nonetheless, as your kids grow, they'll want to chase larger, less numerous quarry, and they'll simply have to learn patience if they want to catch them.

Fishing Helps Keep Kids Out of Trouble

Perhaps the greatest reason out there to take your kids fishing is that the hobby is so time consuming and expensive that if they take to it, they'll never have enough time or money to get hooked on drugs.

You might laugh at that, but it's true: people planning to get up before dawn and spend their whole day in the sun aren't running around until 2:00 a.m. getting hammered. Sometimes, after a full day of fishing I am so tired that even a much-needed shower seems like a chore—the bar is the last thing on my mind!

If "idle hands are the devil's workshop" then what better cure than to fill them with gear to rig up, knots to untangle, and fish to unhook? Further, just as you send your kids off to college to fend for themselves, perhaps they'll take their love of fishing with them and attend one of the many schools that offer fishing programs and even scholarships. This too would send them off to bed timely.

In all honesty, sports in general, and especially fishing, have the chance of keeping your most cherished loved ones healthy and happy in a country plagued by drugs and alcohol. It's a wonderful reason to spend time with your family on the water.

3 – SAFETY

A lot can go wrong while fishing with adults, to say nothing of bringing children along. You can be bitten, hooked, stabbed, cut, jabbed, sliced, burned, dehydrated, drowned or otherwise killed. Taking kids along only makes much of this more likely. Even so, with some basic precautions and forewarning, you should be able to minimize most issues to keep the day safe and happy for everyone.

This isn't the most glamorous chapter – you're probably itching to jump right to the "fun stuff," but this is an important chapter and I suggest you read it. There is a reason I placed it right after the chapters on attitude, and reasons to take your kids fishing. You'll find information in here that ranges from the basics of sun care to little-discussed dangers that can come from certain types of hooks, fishing line, and snags. These aren't things you'd normally think of so please give it a read – it might save you a trip to the hospital.

The Sun

The most likely danger comes from directly overhead – the sun. I've suffered severe sunburns over the years from being too engrossed by fishing to remember to reapply sunscreen timely. The result is never fun, and who knows what sort of long-term damage has been done. This is an easy one to fix, of course – just put on your sunscreen and wear a good hat!

Be extremely careful to apply and reapply sunscreen to your children if they are too young to apply it themselves. They might fuss, but at the end of the day they're counting on you to get them through this process safely, and the decisions you make, or the steps you skip, could come back to haunt them years later. Don't do this to them!

You should also invest in a few pairs of polarized glasses. I say a few because kids have a habit of stepping on them or dropping them off the side of a boat into the water to hear them go "bloop." The glasses serve a few safety purposes. First, they protect against the sun, either directly or from the glare that is on the water. Secondly, and more importantly, they are your only chance against errant hooks cast by little, learning hands. You're an adult – you can take a hook to the arm and deal with it but taking a hook to an eye is something that should be avoided at all cost.

A third benefit to polarized sunglasses has little to do with safety but is a nice perk: they help you see fish and other objects inside the water as they cut down on the sun glare. This is a good thing to remember if your little one doesn't like wearing them – it's a pretty tough sale to convince them to wear them for safety's sake, but you'll find you have infinitely better luck telling them to put on their sunglasses so they can "see the fish."

Life Jackets

When fishing from a boat, or even a rickety dock, life jackets aren't just a good idea – they're often the law. You should read your state's regulations to understand exactly when they must be worn. Some states require that small children always wear life jackets while on a boat, while other states only require them if the boat is underway. I'd suggest taking the more conservative route regardless of state and insist that they be worn while your child is on the boat. Kids are perfectly capable of falling out while the boat is sitting still, and someone else is could crash into your boat at any time as well. Demanding that life jackets be worn at all times will help protect against both of these possibilities and will also minimize the fuss you're likely to receive (the less time they have the life jacket off, the less time they have to realize how much more comfortable it is without one).

On the topic of comfort, I would recommend investing in quality life jackets for your family. This is one area where you really don't want to skimp to save some money. The better the product, the more likely you are to wear it, and a life jacket is only useful when worn. Mustang Survival makes several high-quality life jackets in sizes that will fit anyone from an infant to a grown, obese fisherman. My children have both grown up wearing them and I feel much safer having them in these fine products. They were also great for my kids when they were still toddlers because the infant and child models come with significant padding behind the head, to keep their heads above water automatically if they ever fall in. One side effect I didn't anticipate, but came to love, is that this padding also protects them from falls while they're bumbling about the boat to check out a fish or grab your rod.

While you're shopping for your kids' life jackets, you might also consider purchasing one for yourself. The same company, Mustang Survival, has several personal flotation devices that are auto-inflatable and will deploy automatically once you are submerged in the water. Because they start off "collapsed," they are light weight and very comfortable, which makes it much more likely that you'll wear them. I've been wearing these for years and even on hot days it's hard to remember that it's on sometimes. I can't say enough good things about the product. I will admit they are pricey, but just remember they're protecting something priceless.

If possible, it would be a good idea to take your child to a pool with their life jacket and invest some time in helping them learn how to float in one and right themselves if they flip over. While life jackets are designed to help keep your kid's head above the water, if they're thrashing and terrified, they can upset the buoyancy and get in trouble. As with everything else, experience helps, so spend a little time practicing the important skill of floating.

Hooks – Removing Them from Flesh

If you're allowing your kids to cast, or even to hold the rod while you're trying to release a fish, plan on being accidentally hooked. If this happens to you, it's just the price of admission, but you really don't want this to happen to your kids. It can ruin a trip and add hundreds of dollars to medical bills if you don't know what you're doing.

First off, a disclaimer: I don't recommend doing this with your children unless you have no other choice. With that said, there is a simple way to remove a hook that is embedded beyond the barb, but it's not for the faint of heart. First, you should cut off any other hooks that are near the offending one so that you don't remove one only to jab another into you in the process. Once you do this, you'll want to press the eye of the hook (the part where the line ties in) against your skin and hold it down tight. You'll then take several strands of very heavy line, doubling, tripling or more as necessary and loop it around the bend of the hook (they also sell hook removal tools with heavy-duty line attached and ready). Hold this line in your other hand away and while still applying pressure to the eye, make one short, sharp and strong jerk on the line in the opposite direction of the eye.

By pushing down on the eye, you've angled the barb in such a way that a short burst of pressure should release the hook with minimal injury. Obviously, depending on where the hook goes in, you may or may not be able to handle this yourself. Use your best judgement and seek medical treatment when appropriate. I've had to use this method numerous times on my father as he insists on carrying his tackle in plastic bags that he keeps bunched up in his pockets. They're great products for keeping freshness in, but they aren't intended for treble hooks.

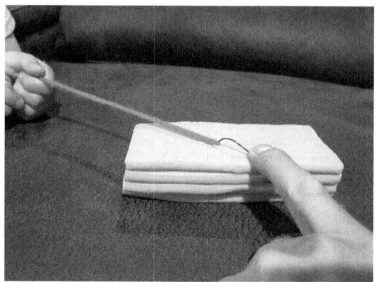

Push down firmly on the eye of the hook to angle the barb in such a way that a quick tug will release it from your friend (or a stick of modeling clay).

Hooks – Preventing Them from Sticking in Flesh

I thought it best to explain how to remove a hook first because if you're sitting on a boat jumping to this section, that's probably what you want to know. With that said, there are a few small steps you can take to prevent the likelihood that there will be a problem in the first place, or at least mitigate the damage it will do.

It makes sense to consider what types of hooks are even necessary to take on the trip, and which ones are more trouble than they're worth. If you're taking small children in a confined area such as a boat or crowded bank, I'd suggest staying away from treble hooks. These are the types of hooks that are commonly found on crankbaits and jerkbaits. They are named treble hooks because there are three "pointy ends" on each. These tend to be the types of hooks that commonly snag people because they are thin, strong, and sharp. Their three-pronged shape also makes it more likely that they'll catch something, as they "stand up" rather than fall flat as other hooks might. Because of these factors, it's very easy for them to embed quickly, deeply and painfully.

While lures with treble hooks are often great at catching fish, all but the smallest models tend to be for larger fish than small children are after, so the trouble and danger may not be worth it. I'd argue that any time you "need" a treble hook lure is probably not the best time to bring a child fishing in the first place. Treble hook lures like jerkbaits and crankbaits tend to be very effective early and late in the year when the water and air are both frigid and aquatic vegetation is less abundant. They still work as the year goes on, of course, but early on it seems like they're the ticket. Perhaps that early in the year is too early for the little ones, anyway.

Leaving treble hooks behind still gives you plenty of options for catching fish, especially once the water starts to warm to the low to mid-sixties. You'll have access to all the panfish hooks that you need, and while these are also generally thin wire, they do have a chance of lying flat and not hooking the skin. To the extent that they do hook, their barbs tend to not be quite as pronounced nor as big of a deal to remove.

When fishing with kids, I prefer using lures with larger single hooks, like spinnerbaits. While it is still possible to snag a person with a larger hook, it is less likely because more force is necessary. It's a bit counter-intuitive, but the larger, scary looking hooks are less likely to catch you than the small and dainty ones. It's much like how a dull knife is more likely to hurt you than a sharp one.

Regardless of what lure you're using, you can also pinch the barbs on your hooks. This won't prevent the hook from accidentally catching a person, but it will minimize the trauma and ordeal if it occurs. The above-mentioned method for hook removal may even prove unnecessary, as without the barb, the hook can easily be backed out. There are some regions, states, and provinces that require barbless hooks for the good of the fish as it is much less traumatic for them as well. There is, of course, some fear that not having a barb will make a fish more difficult to catch, but so long as you keep constant pressure on them, it doesn't seem to make much difference. Just have your kids keep their rod tips high.

Fishing Line

You wouldn't normally think that fishing line would be dangerous to children, but there are a few things that can go wrong. The most common is probably cuts. There are certain types of braided line that are extremely sharp and can deeply cut if forcefully dragged across flesh. This is most likely to happen while a fish is still on the hook. If the fish takes a powerful, jolting run or even flops about haphazardly in the boat while you or your child are holding the line, there is a risk of someone being cut. Pickerel are great at hurting you this way as they tend to flop about madly after being caught.

You can also manage to cut yourself if you run your hand over the line too fast, such as if you go to pull some line past a tightened drag and have your hand slip.

These minor lacerations generally aren't the end of the world, but they can be very painful as they tend to wound the tips of your fingers where all your nerves are. A cut early in the week can put a damper on vacation if it is deep enough, so be aware of the risk. I choose to avoid this risk by using monofilament on my children's rods.

Soft Plastics

Kids would play with soft plastic worms, tubes, and especially salamanders all day long if you would let them, but you need to read the package first because certain brands carry significant health warnings and really shouldn't be handled by children, especially if they still put everything in their mouths. Please make sure you know what you're giving your children so that they don't suffer any long-term ill effects and have them wash their hands when they come back from fishing.

Lead

Please bear in mind that many of the fishing lures out there and most of the weights sold are made of lead. Lead can be harmful to your health, though you'd hope it would take a bit more than some fishing trips to bring about problems. If you're concerned about this, some manufacturers offer alternative tungsten options. These tend to be more expensive, but you're buying peace of mind. In some states, like Massachusetts, they are required by law and one can only expect other states to eventually follow suit.

Snags

You are going to snag lures. A lot of lures. Once your child starts casting on their own, this snag rate is going to explode. You are often going to try and retrieve these lures, and sometimes that's fine and part of fishing. It is vitally important, however, that you use your head when doing so, especially when fishing from a boat. It's one thing to risk your property while heading into shore to retrieve a lure from a tree, but another thing entirely to risk your life when retrieving something from certain underwater snags. I recently had a very scary reminder about this.

I was fishing with my son up on Lake Champlain and we were trolling a grass flat in about 6-7' of water with spinnerbaits. Suddenly, one of the rods bent over and started screaming drag to the point that I had to turn the boat back before the rod was stripped. I wasn't quite sure what to make of it but was hoping that an enormous channel cat had struck, or perhaps a large carp had been foul hooked. I started reeling in an object that wasn't moving much, and eventually got close enough to see that the spinnerbait was embedded in some dock line. Like an idiot, I grabbed the line and started pulling it onto the boat. This dock line was attached to a giant cement boat mooring, long forgotten by its owner. It probably weighed 40-50lb.

I was an idiot because I grabbed the dock line below the spinnerbait, meaning that if my hand slipped, I ran the real risk of also being hooked and dragged immediately overboard. In 6-7' of water with a 50lb weight dragging my hand down, that would have been the end of me. My three-year-old would have seen me go overboard and been helpless and adrift all on his own. It was a stupid, stupid, stupid thing to attempt over an $8 lure. By the grace of God, nothing bad happened, but I got a pretty good shock when the line slipped slightly, and I realized the mistake I was making.

In certain parts of the country, you'll find a heavy line filled with hooks dangling from heavy tree branches near the water. They're often moored by a heavy object below the water, which you can't always see. These are called trotlines, and they can have the same effect as the boat mooring above. Sadly, it's not uncommon for people to drown after becoming tangled in these and dragged overboard, so if you happen to snag one with an errant cast, let discretion rule the day and sacrifice the lure to potentially spare your life.

Clothing

Kids are infatuated by water. They'll head straight for the nearest puddle and merrily splash around all day if you'll let them, and they tend to be enamored by the livewell, even if it has no fish! To put it plainly, if you take your kids anywhere near water (such as when fishing), they're going to find a way to get wet. On an eighty-degree day, that probably doesn't matter much. On a sixty-degree day, it can mean heading home while your kids were still having fun. Plan to bring some spare clothes to avoid an early exit.

Make sure your kids dress in layers to start their day. It's cooler in the mornings than later in the day, and it's not a big deal to shed some layers as the day progresses. Often, they're so excited about fishing that they'll forget to tell you that they're cold until it's too late and they're miserable. The same applies to when they get hot, so check their face for flushing and remove layers as needed.

Rubber boots of some sort are a must as they're easy to clean and allow some missteps. You'll also want a good sun hat that protects from all directions, just in case you miss a spot with the sunscreen. I'd recommend getting one with a good cinching tie to help keep it on their head, and I'd definitely insist that they wear it as a prerequisite to fishing (you can use the same line with the sunglasses – "this is your fishing hat... You can't catch any fish without a fishing hat!").

Rain gear can be important, especially if you're on a boat. Even if the forecast doesn't call for rain, just remember that people don't get to become weathermen until they've killed at least three fishermen, so don't trust a word they say. Even if they do get it right and there's no rain, wind and waves can throw up surf over the bow on a boat, drenching anyone who isn't wearing good rain gear. Remember that your rain gear must be zipped up to work properly – I found that one out the hard way one cold, blustery morning on Lake Champlain!

Gloves are an article of clothing that most people don't think about but can be very useful for kids. I don't mean ones to keep you warm (though those can be nice when it's cooler), but ones that are just meant to give kids a little more confidence when holding fish. They offer some protection from a spine or even the rough mouths that panfish and bass have. While most adult fishermen will view a torn up "bass thumb" as a mark of honor, it can upset small children who tend to want a bandage for every little mark. Gloves will help prevent this and keep them holding the fish nice and steady for photographs.

Holding Fish Safely (For Your Kids)

On that note, we'd better spend a bit of time going over what fish are safe for kids to hold in general. Some fish have an impressive array of fierce teeth, defensive spines and other sharp areas that can injure unaware anglers. Others have substantial bite strength that can bruise little fingers or even toxin-lined jabbers that can leave a good welt. You're going to want to know what you're dealing with before you pass any fish over to your child to hold.

The teeth are simple to identify – look in the fish's mouth and see what you're dealing with. Anything with teeth should never be held by the mouth, and pliers should be used to remove hooks safely.

Many fish have sharp dorsal spines running along the edge of their back that they will instinctively raise when threatened as these make them harder to swallow. While I won't put anything past a young child, I would at least hope they wouldn't try to eat the fish alive. Even so, these spines are just as good at pricking hands as you will find out while unhooking them. It's just part of fishing to be pricked a bit by these spines and your best bet is just to grab the fish and get it over with, but if your child is one who shies easily from pain, you will want to warn them about these spines so they can grab the fish from below or by the mouth instead.

The gill plate is another area that can be sharp, and care should be taken when approaching it as some species are worse than others. The gill plate is the flap of skin that covers the gills. The gills themselves are fragile and should never be touched. While some species, like northern pike, are commonly held by the gill plate, you're probably better off holding these fish for your kids and joining the photo. It's safer for them and for the fish.

Bullhead and catfish have powerful crushing jaws. They aren't strong enough to trouble most adults, but a small thumb could be badly hurt if caught between them. Bullhead also have toxin in the spines of their fins. While the toxin isn't deadly, it does produce incredible pain and a good welt. It's also possible for the spine to break off and embed in your skin, requiring professional medical assistance to remove.

When handling these fish, be aware of the above and avoid placing your hand in front of their dorsal or pectoral fins. The dorsal fin is the one on their back and the pectoral ones are the ones on each side, first back from the eyes. The fish will instinctively raise its spines when removed from the water, so it should be easy enough to locate them. Only the tip of the spine stings, so you can brace the web between your thumb and pointer finger onto the rear edge of the spine. You then need to wrap your remaining fingers on the belly, keeping them behind the pectoral spines.

If you or your kid does end up getting stung by these spines, clean the wound as best you can and apply an antiseptic. It wouldn't be a bad idea to stop at the walk-in on the way home from the lake, either, just to make sure it's cleaned properly and won't become infected.

In general, it's probably not a bad idea to simply tell your children that some fish are "boo boo fish" that only an adult can handle. Kids don't like boo boos and will be pretty good about respecting this rule.

Regardless of the species of fish, it's imperative that you take the hook out before handing it to your child. Otherwise, they're just one random shake away from being hooked themselves.

Holding Fish Safely (For the Fish)

Now that we've spent some time reviewing the dangers handling fish present to the angler, let's go over a few things you need to know about how to handle fish so that you don't endanger them.

The general rule is that you want to touch the fish as little as possible. They have protective slime on them, and when this is wiped off, they are more susceptible to disease. Thus, you don't want to touch a fish more than you must, and it would be better for the fish if you could avoid dropping or dragging it on the floor or dirt. This isn't always avoidable when fishing with children, but it's nice to have a goal.

While you do want to minimize the amount of slime you may potentially rub off, it's still important to properly support the fish when lifting it out of the water or holding it for a photograph. If you are holding a fish by the jaw, you want to avoid holding it an oblique angle where unnecessary stress is placed on its mouth. Instead, you should aim to lift it vertically, as this places less strain on its jaw. If you intend to hold the fish horizontally for whatever reason, please support its belly so that you aren't placing all the pressure right on its mouth. A little slime lost is probably better than breaking its only method of feeding.

Some fish (specifically, the "boo boo fish" discussed above) can't be held by the jaw safely. Instead, you need to either hold them by the back of the head (keeping your fingers away from their eyes) or by placing your fingers between their gills and gill plate, so that you're essentially holding them by the plate. This is not something to have your young kids try, but it's not as tough as it sounds. You do want to make sure that you are not grabbing the gills while you do this, or you could seriously injure the fish.

While learning, it might be best to simply use a net for larger fish. They sell some with a plastic coating on the netting itself that are better for the fish than rope nets and the prices have come down somewhat in recent years. It's also a piece of equipment that you can hold onto for some time and get your money's worth out of.

Hydration & Snacks

It should go without saying that you're going to want to stay hydrated out there. Unless you're bank fishing or have some sort of Bimini top it's very unlikely that there's going to be much shade. You and your kids are both going to work up quite a thirst and you should be ready for this with plenty of spare water. You'll also want to keep plenty of snacks on hand as these will help you all maintain your focus and composure. There is an old fisherman's tale that bananas are bad luck, but they are very handy to pack, especially on a boat, so I go ahead and bring them. I'd argue that I'm more likely to have a bad day without enough food than I am with a banana in the boat.

You will want to remind your children to drink throughout the day because if the fishing goes well enough, they'll forget they're thirsty. You don't want them to get dehydrated out there. This is one of the few things about a fishing trip that you can control easily enough, so control it.

First-Aid Kit

It's a good idea to bring along a first-aid kit with some basic provisions to help you get past minor hiccups in your day. You'll want bandages, anti-septic, some gauze, and likely some over the counter pain relievers. Aloe is never a bad idea in case you miss a spot with the sunscreen, as is chap stick. Many kids will want an ice pack of some sort if they get a boo boo, so either bring along one that activates after crushing, or plan on using the one from the cooler.

An item that you might not think of for your first-aid kit would be good wire-cutting pliers. These are indispensable if you need to cut off a hook quickly. There is going to come a day when you'll be hooked by an errant cast. Depending on the lure that gets you, it might be very important to cut off any adjacent hooks before trying to remove the hook that snagged you, or you'll remove one hook only to find you jabbed yourself with a second.

Boating Safety

If you're fishing from a boat, there are additional safety risks that must be considered. We've already discussed the importance of life jackets above, but drowning isn't the only danger that comes with boating, or even the main concern after someone falls into the water. Many boats have powerful motors, and many falls occur while that powerful motor is running. If the steering wheel is released while the motor is running, the torque of the engine will often put the boat into a circular turn. If you're in the water while your boat is doing this, you are in exceptional danger as you can be hit by your own boat, or the propeller. There is a reason this phenomenon is called "the circle of death."

There is an easy solution to avoid this situation – it's called a kill switch. This switch is attached to a lanyard which should always remain attached to you while the motor is running. If you move too far away from the switch (by choice or accident) the switch will flip, and the motor will shut off. You should make it a point to insist that the driver wear their kill switch when the motor is running. Many life jackets, including the Mustang Survival models that I described above, come with a clip where the kill switch can strongly attach, thus maximizing the life-saving potential of both devices.

Other safety devices include a means of making noise so you can signal for help, flares or other visual signal indicators, fire extinguishers, a flotation device that can be thrown to people in the water, and a good radio for calling for help. Many of these items are part of the minimum federal safety equipment requirements. I hesitate to list the exact requirements here as they may be subject to change and I wouldn't want to steer you wrong, but you can locate current requirements at the U.S. Coast Guard Boating site: https://www.uscgboating.org.

Another handy reference available on the site is a sample "Float Plan." To put it plainly, someone ought to know where you are heading, who you are going with, and when you plan to return or check in. You want to leave this information with a reliable person that you can trust to call the Coast Guard if you don't check in or return as planned. The last thing you want to do is be adrift for days because no one knew when to expect you.

Other Resources

If you're interested in learning more about safety, there are some great resources available on the internet that you should explore further. The U.S. Coast Guard https://www.uscgboating.org/ discussed above and the Boat U.S. Foundation https://www.boatus.org are two great sites with plenty of safety tips, and links to boater safety courses. I'd certainly recommend a boater safety course even if you don't own a boat just yet. After all, knowing that what your buddy is doing is crazy is just as important as knowing not to do it yourself.

Make safety a priority while you're out there. Somebody loves you and needs you, and that person might be fishing next to you. Just think back to how you felt before your first kid was born. I'll bet many of you signed up for an Infant CPR class and read what you could about common ailments and dangers. Apply the same caution – it doesn't mean you can't have fun, but it will help you make sensible choices that may avert disaster.

4 – USEFUL SKILLS & TRICKS

Unless you're a true glutton for punishment, I'd recommend that you and your children learn some basic skills before you head anywhere near the water. As the "fishing guide," you are going to need to know how to handle some common situations, and as the primary "client," your children are going to want to have at least a basic grasp of the concept of fishing and how a rod and reel work before you hand them one. This chapter will also include some tips on how to acclimate very young children (less than two-years-old) to some of these basic skills so you can get your family out on the water and making memories as quickly as possible.

Two Basic Knots

You're not going to get very far with fishing if you can't tie some simple knots. You want to tie these correctly, because if you don't, you're setting yourself up for failure the moment a big fish strikes. There's a host of things that can go wrong while fighting a fish, but a properly-tied knot is within your control, so as stated before – control it!

There are plenty of books written exclusively on different fishing knots and they're filled to the brim with different options for different situations. Taking nothing away from them (they do have their advantages), I'm trying to keep things simple here, and you can get by just fine with two simple knots for most situations: the Uni Knot, and the Palomar Knot. In fact, I'd go so far as to say you could use the Uni Knot exclusively, but the Palomar Knot is key to tying a drop shot, which is going to be one of your main techniques while targeting panfish with your children.

The Uni Knot

The Uni Knot is useful for tying most lures. If you're using braid (against my advice from the safety chapter might I add!) then the Uni Knot works extremely well, but it will also work with monofilament and fluorocarbon. Its main advantages are that it's very simple to tie and is ideal for joining two lines together (such as when you want a leader). I've found myself employing it for broken shoelaces and other non-fishing-related string as well.

To tie the Uni Knot, pass your line through the eye of a hook, fold it back against itself and form a loop (figure 1). Spiral the tag line around this loop (figure 2). You'll want to do this 5-7 times if attaching your line to your lure, but 3-4 times will work if attaching your line to the spool. Once you've done this, hold the main line above the knot and pull the tag end to cinch the knot tight. If done correctly, it will coil tightly like a snake ready to strike (figure 3). Once your line is tightened, hold onto the main line above the hook and the hook itself and pull the main line tight, drawing the "coiled snake" to the eye of the hook (figure 4).

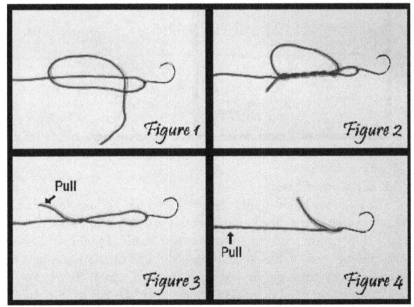

The Uni Knot

You can also tie a Double Uni Knot to attach two lines together. This is handy for adding more line to a spool after a particularly bad tangle or adding a leader.

Basically, you're tying two Uni Knots. Lay two lines of roughly equal diameter flat and running parallel to each other, and make an overhead loop crossing each other (figure 1). Spiral the tag end of each line around each loop, just as you would in a single Uni Knot (figure 2). Pull each tag end taut, to "coil the snake" (figure 3). I suggest doing this one at a time for simplicity. Finally, pull each main line at the same time to bring the two "coiled snakes" together (figure 4). Trim any excess tag lines.

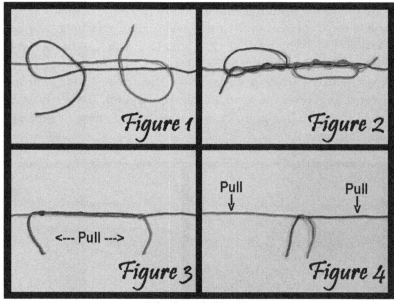

The Double Uni Knot

The Palomar Knot

The Palomar Knot is also very simple to tie. So simple in fact that there is a joke among fishermen that this is the only knot the bass guys know how to use, and the only one they need. Tying one is simple: Pass the tag end of the line through the eye of the hook and then double it back through the eye again to form a loop (figure 1). The size of loop you need depends on the size of the lure you're using, as you'll soon see. Make an overhead knot on the doubled line while letting the lure dangle below from the middle (figure 2). Finally, pass your lure through the doubled tag line (figure 3) and tighten the line down until is snug against the eye of the lure (figure 4). You'll want to wet the knot with saliva or water before tightening it to reduce friction.

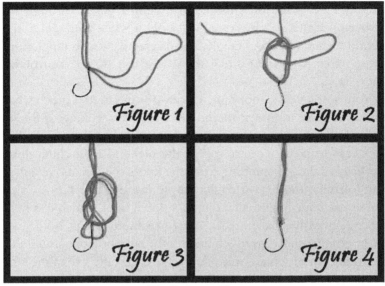

The Palomar Knot

When finished, snip off any remaining tag end unless you're tying a drop shot, in which case tie a sinker to the tag end instead. You do need to make sure that your hook faces up, and although there's a "perfect" way to tie the knot that will allow this, the easy, less confusing way is simply to check and see if the hook point is facing up when you hold the main line and tag end taut. If the hook is pointing down, run the tag end of the line through the eye of the hook again from the top to the bottom to turn it as desired.

Spooling Line

Now that you know how to tie a knot, you're going to want to spool some line onto your reel. Many tackle shops will do this for you if you bring the reel in and purchase line from them, but it's not rocket science.

Again, we'll suppose that you're starting with a spinning reel. It seems simple enough at first glance – just tie the line to your spool and start reeling it in, right? For the most part, yes, but you do want to make sure that the line is leaving the filler spool in the opposite direction that your bail is spinning. Since spinning reels turn clockwise, this means you want the line coming off counterclockwise. Lay the filler spool flat on the ground to achieve this, and simply flip it over if the line is leaving the wrong way.

Many folks make the mistake of poking a pencil through the reel and having someone else (or a vice) hold it while they reel it in. This will lead to line twist and tangles. Kids create enough tangles on their own, so this is another small thing you can do to control what is controllable.

From a practical standpoint, it really doesn't matter much what type of knot you use to attach the line to your reel, so long as the knot is small and holds strong. Some people make a little noose or slip knot as it's easy to pass over the top of the reel and then cinch down. If your head is already spinning from the knots section above and you're done learning knots, you could simply use the Uni Knot. You will need to use your fingernail to cinch it down tight, which can be a little challenging with smaller reels, but once there it will hold just fine. You're going to have so much line on the spool that it shouldn't cause any trouble, but I would only use 3 or so coils rather than the standard 5-7, just to reduce the size of the knot.

Take care not to overfill your spool or you could cause yourself some headaches with tangles. You'll want to leave about a 1/8" gap between the line and the lip of your spinning reel. You'll also want to ensure that the line is wrapped tightly because if you don't, you're setting yourself up for wind knots which will be discussed in the "Dealing with Tangles" section of this chapter.

If using braid, bear in mind that it tends to "slip" on reels if spun directly onto them. Many reels come advertised as "braid-ready," and you'll see that they have little rubber lines running up or down the spool to prevent the braid from slipping. You can achieve the same effect by spooling on a "backing" of monofilament. Once you've reeled on a few layers of this, attach it to the braid with the Double Uni Knot and you won't have to worry about your line slipping. An added benefit is you'll save money as you won't have to use as much expensive braid.

Casting a Spinning Reel

To cast your spinning rod, take the line that is leaving your reel and hold it with your pointer finger. You then flip the bail of the reel, pull back the rod with your wrists and then accelerate them forward, releasing the line from your finger when the tip of your rod is facing where you want the lure to go. Once the lure splashes down in the water, close the bail. While reeling will close the bail automatically, it's better for the reel to do this manually by flipping it shut with your other hand. This will increase the life expectancy of this expensive equipment.

It should go without saying that before casting you want to make sure that no one is in your way. When your child is learning how to cast, you'd do very well to stand to their side and slightly behind them, away from the rod.

You can cast several different ways, with overarm (raising the rod tip up above your head vertically), sidearm (moving the rod tip to the side of your body horizontally), and underarm (moving the rod tip lower than your wrists and then raising it to cast) being the simplest.

Sidearm is probably the safest and you can still generate significant distance once you get the hang of things. Overarm is best for distance and with practice an underarm cast tends to be the most accurate. There are other techniques such as pitching and flipping but these are beyond the scope of this book as they are more than you need to know to successfully take your child fishing. If interested, an internet search will yield ample information.

Casting a Spincast Reel

If you find that your child struggles too much with a spinning reel and can't overcome the difficulty, spincast reels are, admittedly, easier for them to cast. All they need to do is press and hold the button (usually on the bottom of the reel) and then start their cast. When the tip of the rod is in the direction that they want the lure to fly, they release the button, which then releases the lure. Cranking the reel handle then reengages the locking mechanism so the lure can be cast again.

If you do choose a spincast reel, at least get one that might last a few trips. There are plenty of little "gimmick" rods and reels out there on the market, but these are just that – gimmicks. I am convinced they exist solely to have your children ask you to buy them. Ask the sales associate for a high-quality spincast reel rather than the plastic stuff. While plenty of people go completely overboard with their fishing tackle selections, you don't want to get the least expensive option, either. As with everything else in life, you get what you pay for.

Casting a Baitcast Reel

I know that at least one of you out there is going to try to start your kid off with a baitcast reel. This will be against all the advice you'll find in the world's tackle shops, on the internet, and in this book. Don't say I didn't warn you, but if you're going for it, there's a few things you ought to know.

Baitcast reels can be a pain for even professionals because they tend to backlash. What happens is that the spool spins faster than the line releases from it in a cast, and this can cause an enormous tangle. It's not uncommon to go through several thousand yards of line while learning how to cast these reels, hence it's not recommended at all for children.

Still reading? Well, OK then. You cast a baitcast reel by clicking the spool release button with your thumb. This will cause line to unravel from the spool, so you need to place this same thumb on the spool itself to stop it from unwinding. You then begin your casting motion, and when the tip of your rod is facing where you want the lure to go, you release your thumb from the spool. The lure will now take off through the air, and the spool will be moving as line is stripped from it. As your lure approaches the water, you'll want to thumb the spool a bit to slow its descent, and really clamp down tight just as it hits the water.

If you don't do this, the spool will continue to move just as fast as it was moving while traveling through the air, but the increased resistance from the water will slow the lure quickly once it splashes down. This means that the line will no longer be stripped at the same rate, causing a backlash. The same principle of resistance applies when casting into the wind, so you'll need to thumb the spool throughout the lure's flight to avoid a backlash.

The chances of a young kid figuring this all out are slim to none, and bad backlashes are among the worst tangles you can deal with, so—again—I do not recommend handing your child a baitcaster in the first place. If you insist on doing so, one small thing you can do to reduce everyone's frustration is to take off about as much line as you figure they can cast, and then put some tape down on the remaining line on the spool. This way, if there is a backlash, it should stop at the tape and be small and manageable. At worst you'll only have to cut out a bit of line – not respool your entire reel.

Dealing with Tangles

It won't be long after you hand a fishing rod over to your child that they manage to tangle it somehow. It would be wise to coach them to tell you about these as soon as possible because the longer they go unfixed, the worse the become. Even if they do tell you immediately (and young kids probably won't), you'll want to bring along at least two rods as you'll likely spend much of your day untangling the other.

Some tangles are pure works of art – a crazy web of monofilament jutting out from every direction with no defined flow or form – almost like a frustrating, hair-greying form of jazz. There's not much you can do about these monstrosities. If you enjoy puzzles and have all the time in the world, you might be able to restore order to many tangles, but with kids you have no time at all – you're in a race against the clock because every second they have a fishing rod in their hand is another second closer to the next tangle. Given this, it's often best to simply cut your losses (and the line) if things get totally out of hand.

Other tangles are simple, common, and easy to resolve if you know what you're doing but can be somewhat perplexing at first. The more common situations include line that becomes buried and stuck in the underside of the spinning spool, line that forms a wind knot on the spool itself, and line that becomes spiraled over the fishing rod eyes.

Kids manage to get a lot of line stuck inside the rotating spool of spinning reels. If you catch it quickly enough, you may simply be able to gently pull it out the opposite direction it entered, but if this isn't working, chances are that it has caught on the inside gearing mechanism. This sounds worse than it is. Most spinning reels have a knob on top which is called the drag. Loosening this knob will eventually cause the spool to detach from the main reel body, revealing the tangled mess inside. You may be able to unwind the line at this point, or you may need to cut it. If it looks badly kinked and frayed there's not much point in trying to save it, so cut off and start over.

Spinning reels tend to form wind knots. These tangles form on the line itself – you'll notice them as you'll feel some resistance as you cast or retrieve, and a balled-up section of line pulls through the rod's eyes. Wind knots are caused by slack forming in the line that is laying in the reel. As a cast is made, this slack can sometimes catch itself and the outgoing line, which can lead to trouble.

The best way to prevent wind knots is simply to avoid them in the first place by keeping line taut on the reel, but if they do form, you need to assess the situation and determine if it's possible to untangle quickly, or if it's so tight that you're going to need to cut the line. You can usually untangle these if you catch them quickly enough and choose the right end of the line to tug on – they'll unravel themselves. If you choose the wrong one, you'll find the knot tightening down until it becomes impossible to untangle, so tread carefully.

Another common situation you'll run into is a little perplexing at first: you or your child will be reeling in the lure and you'll find that it's slow going. If you look towards the tip of the rod, you will see the culprit: the line has formed a spiral loop around one of the guides. The first time you see it can be confusing to understand how to fix it, but it's the simplest of cures. Pull the line out away from the rod to form a loop. You should now see that it can be fixed by passing the lure through that loop. At least something was easy!

Regardless of how the tangle formed, if you manage to straighten it out, you'll still want to take a good look at the line and assess if it appears scraped, kinked, or otherwise damaged, as all of these will reduce its strength. If you think you've done more harm than good untangling the line, you'll want to retie before a big fish tests that weakened line and dashes your kid's dreams!

Backlashes

As mentioned earlier, if you are letting your kids mess around with a baitcaster reel, you're going to run into backlashes. I've already discussed how they form but here's how you untangle them: if you took my advice and put some tape down as discussed above (which I'm kind of doubting, since you are using a baitcaster in the first place), then the backlash shouldn't be that bad. You can probably fix it by pressing the spool release button so line will feed out, and then slowly stripping it by hand until the backlash has left the reel and each revolution of the spool shows neat line. If you reach a point where the line won't pull out, it's because it's tangled within the spool. You'll see a loop or fold where it's caught. You need to pick at this loop until the line releases from its grip and can be pulled from the spool. If the backlash is particularly bad, throw the whole combo in your rod locker, pick up a spinning rod instead, and start paying attention to the advice in this book!

Hooking & Fighting Fish

So, you've gotten to the lake with a spooled reel, dealt with ten or twenty tangles, and have managed to cast out some bait. Suddenly, you feel a tug – there's a fish! Great! Now what? Well, the first thing you need to do is make sure the fish is hooked. You do this by "setting" the hook. Depending on what type of hook, there are different techniques, but most of them call for snapping the rod back away from the fish suddenly to drive the hook through its mouth. The exception is a circle hook, where you simply reel in (they are designed so that doing this will hook the fish in the corner of its mouth as it attempts to swim away).

If the hook's point is not inside the fish's mouth, there is a good chance that you'll pull the bait away while setting the hook, so you do want to wait until you're fairly certain they actually have it before you start. Even so, don't wait too long as they'll either figure out that something is wrong and spit out the hook, or swallow it (neither of which you want).

If you don't hook the fish while fishing with bait, just lower the rod tip again and allow the bait to start falling again. Panfish often travel in schools and are very competitive for food, so other nearby fish will view this morsel as something that "escaped" from their peer and pounce on it. Further, if the initial fish never actually felt the hook, there's a chance it too will continue to chase the bait.

Soon enough, you'll manage to hook a fish (you'll know this because your line will dart wildly in the water as the fish starts tugging madly, trying to escape). If you're fishing with small children, now's the time to tell them that there's a fish on the line so they can come over to try and reel it in. You always want to keep pressure on the fish and a bend in the rod while waiting for them to run over and while handing them the rod. Any slack in the line will give the fish a good chance to spit the hook and escape, leaving your little one with nothing but a minor dose of disappointment. This will, unfortunately, happen from time to time, so it's important to be prepared for it and just keep on smiling and let out a big "Oh well!" You don't want to make them feel like they failed, especially if it has been awhile between bites.

Assuming the handoff goes well, and the fish remains on the line, it's now time to coach your child through reeling it in. I've noticed that very small children tend to drop the rod tip and point it right at the fish so there is no bend in the line at all. So long as it's a small fish and they're reeling fast enough to keep the pressure on, this isn't the end of the world, but it's a terrible habit will cost them a larger fish eventually. First, it's challenging to keep pressure on the fish in this way, and secondly, without any bend in the rod, you're putting all the pressure on the line instead of the rod and really testing that line strength. A large fish will snap the line.

A good way to avoid this and coach your child through is to tell them to "keep the rod tip high!" Now, if you watch the pros, you'll see they often don't do this because they don't want the fish to jump. Instead, they'll often keep the rod tip very low but angled so there is still a bend in the rod. This is harder to coach to and impractical for younger children as keeping the rod tip low for them means keeping it below the gunwale (the top edge of the side of a boat), or down in the dirt when fishing from shore. So, "keep your rod tip high!" is going to have to do. This will lead to some spectacular jumping sequences, especially with smallmouth bass, which can lead them to throw the hook now and then, but at least they'll give a good show in the process.

While your kid is fighting the fish, keep encouraging them and telling them what a great job they're doing. You're probably going to have to remind the littlest ones to "reel, reel, reel" now and then, which they'll tend to do with a huge smile on their face and tons of giggles.

If the fish is strong enough, you may hear it take off line. This sounds like "zzzzziiiiip!" as line is stripped from the reel. Ideally, you don't want to reel while this is happening, as that causes line twist. Good luck getting a toddler to stop, but you can try coaching them just to "let the fish take some line" while they hold the rod tip high. When the "zzzzziiiiip!" sound stops, it's time to start reeling again.

If a larger fish approaches shore or the boat, it's important to ensure that your child does not attempt to lift it straight from the water as that can cause the line to break. You'll either want to net the fish or grab it by hand instead. It's also important that your child not reel fish (of any size) in so high that they touch the tip of the rod. This can dislodge the hook or even break the rod. Kids don't know when to stop reeling so it's important that you're there to guide them.

Landing Fish

When your child has their first large fish on the line your heart is likely racing a mile a minute, dreading all the things that might go wrong. It's normal to want your children to be successful, after all, and a lot of hard work went into this moment! You might have a lump in your throat as the fish gets closer and closer and you're probably only thinking of getting it up on shore safely before it can get away and you lose your photo and memory.

As much as I and everyone else out there will tell you not to do this, you or your kid will probably drag that poor fish right up on the shore, through the sand or brush, as far away from the water as you can, lest it jump and spoil the day. Well, you're going to do this the first time because it's normal to put your kids first, and I'm not going to beat you up about it. Even so, do realize that this is terrible for the fish's health and should never be the goal, or become routine. Instead, try to minimize how much and where the fish is touched by anything, including hands.

It's important to do this because many species of fish have a protective slime coat on them that helps them guard against infection and disease. Excessive touching can remove this slime, leaving them less likely to survive upon release. They're also just as capable as any other creature of being banged up and bruised if handled roughly or dragged across a pebbly shore. Even if you were intending to keep and eat the fish, this isn't going to help its taste.

A much better approach is to land the fish by hand or net in the water, grab it safely as described in Chapter 3, unhook it and then hand it to your child for a quick photo before sending it on its way.

If you're going to invest in a net, it would be better if you spent a little extra money (typically another $20-$30) to invest in a net with a rubber (or at least rubber coated) mesh as opposed to nylon. This is better for you, because hooks are much less likely to become snagged in the net, and better for the fish, because the rubber coating is designed to take it easy on their protective slime and fins. It's still touching these, of course, but it's a balancing act between touching the fish with the net or potentially hurting the fish (and/or yourself) while landing it by hand while it's thrashing.

Unhooking Fish

Parents should not allow young children to unhook fish, because if the fish is not held firmly during the process and shakes, there is a chance that the hook will leave the fish's mouth and enter the child's

47

hand – never fun.

Unhooking fish isn't always easy for adults, either. While it's not a big deal to remove a hook that's near the opening of the fish's mouth, things get trickier when the hook is taken deeper or swallowed.

As a rule, unhook fish whenever you can do so without further injuring them. Sometimes, the hook is taken so deeply that efforts to remove it do more harm than good. It's not much fun for anyone to see an animal in distress and bleeding.

The best way to prevent this is to arrive at the lake with barbless hooks as they're much easier to remove from fish (and hands) as indicated in Chapter 3. They're significantly easier on the fish and legally required in some areas (and likely more in the future). You'll also want to use hooks with a long shank when fishing for panfish as it's much easier to remove a hook if you can grab at least part of it outside of the mouth to leverage. Unfortunately, even if you take both precautions, some hooks will still be difficult to remove.

The first thing you need to do is assess the situation and understand just what you're dealing with. Is the hook against the wall of the cheek, but just deeper? Is it hooked against the gills? Has part of it been swallowed? Different situations compel different remedies.

If the hook is against the wall of the cheek, it might be as simple as getting out a good set of needle nose pliers and going in after it. If you're dealing with a chain pickerel, northern pike, or other toothy critter, a good set of mouth spreaders can really help. This metal tool is designed to keep the jaw open so that you can safely and quickly work inside it and remove deeper hooks.

If the hook is in the gills, you need to decide fast as this is a very fragile area for the fish. You don't want to rip the hook out as part of the gill is going to come with it. Sometimes you'll find that the hook isn't embedded in the gill, but just tightened against it (the bottom of the "U" of the hook is locked against the gill). In these cases, giving the line some slack will cause it to fall away. The trick is getting it past the gills after it falls. Depending on the size of the fish, you might not have much room between each gill, so if you can get it to fall out of the gill plate (meaning it's now on the outside of the fish) do the poor thing a favor and just cut your line and retie. Don't risk injuring the fish by trying to pass the hook back through the gills to spare yourself another knot. After all the tangles and snags you've dealt with you should be an expert at tying knots by now, anyway!

If the hook is embedded in the gill, and it won't slide out easily, you should see if it's possible to reach the barb (if you're using one) and snap it off with a pair of wire cutters. Having these in different sizes is obviously helpful here. Cutting the barb will allow you to remove the hook from the gill and likely save the fish's life. A fish is much more likely to recover from a small puncture to its gill than from having part of it ripped out.

Fish that have swallowed the hook completely are another matter. If you can't even see it, there's not much else you can do except cut the line. The fish may pass the hook, figure out a way to regurgitate it, or simply deal with it as best it can, but it's better to do this than try tugging on it and doing who-knows-what damage to its internal organs in the process.

Sometimes you can still see part of the hook, as it has only been partially swallowed. There is a technique that can often be used to safely remove the hook in such situations. Your objective is to get the bend of the hook facing towards the fish's mouth so that you can pull it from the bend rather than from the eye. To do this, you'll want to cut the line leaving about six inches from the eye. Pass this line through the gill plate and the first set of gills and grab it with your other hand. Pull gently to change the angle of the hook, causing the bend to point up. You should now be able to enter the mouth with longer needle nose plyers, grab the bend, and remove the hook.

Some people will tell you that if you leave the hook inside the fish, it will rust out. It seems doubtful that some modern hooks are going to do this timely, but even if this does eventually happen, the fish must hunt and eat in the meanwhile. You should certainly try your best to remove hooks whenever possible and if it seems truly unlikely that you can do so without mortally wounding the fish, you might want to consider keeping that fish for a meal where legal rather than release it to struggle and suffer.

Acclimating Children to the Task at Hand

So far, we've discussed many skills that you will need before setting off on your first fishing adventure with your kids, but your children also need a little prep work to make the trip successful.

My son was out on the boat learning about fish before he turned one and was casting and hooking his own small fish before he turned two. Granted, he wasn't going to win any awards for distance or accuracy, but if you put him near a school of panfish he could cast to them, hook them, and reel them in, much to my bewilderment and pride. I like to think he has an innate talent for this, but nurture had just as much to do with this as nature.

I exposed him to fishing as soon as possible. He was born in June, and by the following Memorial Day, I had him set up with a life jacket and was taking him out on boat rides. The objective here was not for him to catch any fish, but to watch me catch fish while his mother played with him (she is a Saint). He couldn't even walk yet, so catching fish was totally out of the question, but children start learning from a very young age so I would talk to him about the fish, hold them up for him to lightly touch so he could understand they weren't scary, and generally just make a big exciting deal out of the whole situation. I was trying to get him acclimated to being on the water in a life jacket, and excited about fishing (it worked).

We live in the north, so the open water season is fleeting. As summer turned to fall and then winter, I went and bought him a small ice fishing rod that he could play with inside. I took the hooks off a crankbait and tied it to this rod and cast it across the living room and showed him how to "reel, reel, reel!" Soon, I was handing it to him and having him do the reeling while telling him to "keep your rod up high!" We made a game out of watching the crankbait scurry across the floor, and after a while I would start tugging back on the crankbait pretending to be a "fishy." The goal here was to get him used to the motion of reeling in the line and keeping a bend in the rod by keeping it raised—two skills he'd need when the water opened, and we started fishing again for real.

Once there was open water, I took him out fishing (and by "open water" I mean the first warm week in February, which was foolish as I was very fortunate to catch something—you really want the first time to be successful and I was taking a chance). I managed to hook a small bass and handed him the rod to reel it in, once again saying "reel, reel, reel" and "keep your rod up high!"

As the weather warmed, I stopped being such an overeager fool and started doing some of the scouting homework and site preparation that we will discuss in Chapter 7 so that we would be more likely to have success. I still did most of the casting, presenting, and hooking, but he was doing all the reeling at this stage. As I had improved at my preparations, and was putting him on more and more fish, he was doing a lot of reeling at this stage and became completely enamored with the sport.

It didn't take him very long to flex his independence and want to learn how to cast on his own. We were using spinning rods which made the job a bit difficult for him at first as his hands are too small to cast them as intended, but he proved a resourceful little devil and figured out that he could simply use two hands instead of one. Fish soon came on their own and he was able to truly say he had caught them "all by himself." Even so, that never stopped him from running over to steal my rod when I hooked one!

As of writing, he has just turned four and he continues to cast his own rod with increasing distance and accuracy. We've been playing a game lately where I brought a large cardboard box outside and set it up about 20 feet away from our deck which is raised about 1' off the ground. We take turns seeing who can cast a lure into the box first.

I do credit this acclimation process with helping my son achieve a remarkable degree of fishing independence from a very young age. It was great fun for both of us, improved his motor skills and confidence, and helped to set him up for success with this sport. If your significant other doesn't have the fishing gene, they might think you're crazy, but this process works.

5 – GEAR AND TACKLE

There are few sports out there as geared towards marketing as fishing. Every professional's boat has as many stickers and endorsements on it as an average stock car, and there is no shortage of fishermen willing to endorse this brand or that. The amount of choice out there is astronomical, which is especially daunting as you're getting started.

We can cut through most of the tackle store in one sentence: all you really need to catch fish with your kids are a rod, reel, line, hook, sinker, and bait. That's right: six items. These six items will enable you to tie a "drop shot" which is the only rig that you actually "need" to put your kids on fish.

Even if you want to expand your horizons and try other lures, you don't need to be overwhelmed by choice, or break the bank. Indeed, you should purchase a few types of lures that can cover a variety of situations and purchase less expensive versions of them as your kids will soon rocket them towards the nearest tall tree, anyway. There is absolutely no need to mortgage your home on a wide assortment of rods, reels, or lures while your children are getting started, and less can be more as they are learning.

With that said, you also don't want to purchase the cheapest stuff you can find, because there is a reason for the low price. As with most things in life, if you buy the cheapest option the first time, you'll find yourself upgrading by choice or necessity soon. You want your purchases to make sense and last more than a few hours, so strike a balance between price and quality.

In this chapter, I'll write a few tips to help you navigate the multitude of options out there and make a wise decision, but before I do anything else, let me explain why the drop shot is the ultimate kid-friendly fishing lure. Knowing this will help explain why you should purchase gear that supports this technique before you purchase anything else.

Dropshot – The Ultimate Kid-Friendly Lure

The dropshot is hands down my favorite rig to give to my son. It is the old faithful that I know will always catch fish, no matter where I am, and is a lure that I've used to catch everything from the tiniest bluegill to massive carp. I have caught both my smallest and largest freshwater fish on this technique.

What Kind of Fish Do Dropshots Catch?

A dropshot will catch everything in the lake, though it can take some skill to land larger fish because you're usually using lighter line and a smaller hook, so if you try to horse in a large fish, there's a great chance that the line will snap or the hook will bend over.

I've caught bluegill, sunfish, white perch, smallmouth bass, largemouth bass, chain pickerel, northern pike, freshwater drum and carp on dropshots. Smallmouth especially seem to favor the technique as they tend to like any minnow-shaped bait, as many dropshot baits are.

You can tell that a dropshot is great for fishing with kids because so many professional bass fishermen complain about the technique. While they love the fact that they can catch huge bass with one, they are often frustrated because they must weed through so many little fish before they find a large one. This is music to a parent's ears.

When I'm out with my kids, I couldn't care less about catching a bass. All I want to do is catch as many panfish as possible, and a dropshot is perfect for that. In fact, little fish will hit a drop shot so aggressively that when fishing by myself, I often use this technique as a barometer of sorts to test for signs of life. If I don't feel little fish tapping away at it soon, I know I need to keep moving.

How Do You Fish a Dropshot?

Dropshots can be fished with either live bait or soft plastics. They are one of the few presentations where it doesn't seem matter what you choose, so if you have moral qualms about using live bait, pick up a pack of artificial minnows and have a guilt-free ball.

My favorite way to fish a dropshot is just to cast it out into the wind or current and then let it sink down. I let it drop all the way to the bottom and then I just hold my rod off to the side slightly to keep the line taut enough that I can detect bites. When I feel a fish has the hook, I sweep my rod backward with some authority to set the hook.

I find this to be a great way to fish because the current or wind gives action to the lure, and I can keep it dangling in prime real estate for a long time until a fish comes over to nab it.

I know my local lakes well, so I have a good idea of where most of the underwater boulders and other cover are at some of my favorite spots. Fishing a dropshot allows me to make a cast to one side or the other of cover and then leave the lure there.

This is a very effective way to catch fish, and a great way for kids to fish because it's "cast it and forget it." I'll often pitch a drop shot near some cover and then put the rod in a holder and wait for it to bend while sharing a peanut butter and jelly sandwich with my son. The natural movement of water, especially in wind or current, gives the lure all the action it needs without any input from me.

If there isn't any wind or current, or if I'm walking a bank somewhere, I like to just make ever so slight taps of the lure by raising my rod tip slightly 3-4 times and then reeling in slack, just as I might do with a plastic worm. This gives a little action to the lure and I've found that to be more effective.

When and Where to Fish a Dropshot?

I will fish a dropshot just about anywhere that I can find clear water. It's not a great technique for fishing in heavy weeds but can be great if you cast just next to them, as fish will dart out from the cover to have a bite.

It's also a very good choice if you need or wish to fish deep as it will sink all the way to the bottom if you let it. I will fish it completely vertically under my boat just picking off the fish that show up on the sonar, which is a fun trick to show your kids as it almost turns fishing into a video game for them.

Although you could rig the actual bait weedless and throw it into heavy cover, there's just too much going on with the line and sinker, so if you throw it into cover you're going to lose a lot of gear or get fouled too often.

But who am I kidding? You're going to get fouled all the time regardless of where you throw it. This is a definite drawback of dropshots and the reason why sinkers made for the technique are designed to break away.

It's fair to say that any technique that is designed to touch bottom has a very high chance of never returning to the surface. You will find yourself re-tying constantly throughout the day even if you're fishing by yourself, much less taking along kids and throwing in all the tangles and hazards they bring. This is certainly a drawback, but worthwhile when you consider how well the technique works.

Recap

While it does stink that you'll lose many sinkers and retie many times, of all the lures I've used, there is nothing that will catch as many fish for your kids as this technique. It's just about perfect in so many ways:

- Dropshots have a single hook that is safer for kids than treble hooks.
- They catch every type of fish in the lake and if you bait them appropriately, they'll catch them often.
- They let you quickly appreciate if you're in a good spot, because if you don't feel any taps soon, there's an issue.
- They are easy for kids to cast because the sinker has enough weight to it that it will carry well.
- They work very well with the ultralight fishing rods that little kids are prone to use.
- They can be "cast it and forget it" in that they'll catch fish even if they're just sitting there (especially if they're tipped with worms).
- They're adaptable – removing the weight is a pinch if you aren't getting bit. Sometimes fish want the worm to fall slower, and you can adjust the presentation to test this theory within seconds and without retying.

It's very important to me that you have a successful fishing trip with your kids. The dropshot should put your kids on some fish and get you a few smiling photographs to send to the grandparents.

Start by baiting it with a nightcrawler and go from there. If you don't feel taps within about 30 seconds, move around a bit and cast somewhere slightly different. This will work, or at the very least tell you what areas don't hold fish.

I've loved the dropshot technique long before my children were born and bought my most expensive rod (though you certainly don't need one) specifically for this presentation. I can't say enough good things about it.

Now that I've regaled you with the wonders of the drop shot, let's look at six items that you need to put the rig together – rod, reel, line, hook, sinker, and bait. After that, I'll discuss a few other lures that you might want to try with your kids, but let's start with the basics.

Rod & Reel Combos

It can be tempting to go buy your son or daughter that cute little "first fishing rod" setup with the princess or superhero on it. They tend to come with a rod and reel combo, and many even come with a little tackle box filled with lures. I'd pass. These usually aren't the best quality and the same companies that manufacture them have much better offerings for just a few dollars more. While there isn't anything "wrong" with these setups, I would expect you'll be buying another rod soon, as many of these setups are better described as toys.

Another issue with the toy combos is that (for the most part at least) they tend to either have spincast reels or spinning reels that are oversized for little hands. While there's nothing inherently wrong with spincast reels (some kids find them easier to cast), you're unlikely to find many applications for them throughout life, so you're buying equipment that you might not get much use out of down the road. I try to get my money's worth out of my gear, so I prefer to buy stuff that I envision my son using his entire life.

For these reasons, I'd recommend spending slightly more money than you would on the princess rod and getting a proper setup, either by finding a bit more robust rod and reel combo, or by purchasing the rod and reel separately. Buying a combo tends to be less expensive, but they're also one size fits all, so I prefer to mix and match my own rods and reels. This requires knowing a bit about rods and reels, what to look for, and how they are sized.

Fishing Rods

If you go to your local tackle shop and look through the fishing rods, you'll see that most of them have labels on them near the reel seat that describe their length, power, and action. Different manufacturers offer a wide variety of rods that have different attributes and are useful in different situations. The type of rod that is best for you depends on the size of your children and the species of fish you're trying to catch.

The length of the rod is the most self-explanatory part of the label. A 5'6" rod is exactly that – 5'6". Smaller is generally better for younger children as they don't always have the strength to lift a larger rod and keep the tip high while fighting fish. Shorter rods have other advantages in that they tend to be easier to cast accurately, and easier to use in tighter quarters (such as beneath trees on a wooded bank of your local pond). Their disadvantages are that they tend to struggle with heavier lures, require more skill to land large fish with, and don't cast as far as a longer rod.

A rod's power is a measurement of how heavy or stout it is – in other words, how resistant it is to bend. They range from extra-heavy power to ultra-light power. Heavier rods are used to target larger species, throw larger lures, and drag fish out of thicker cover. It takes more effort to bend them, which is useful when casting heavy lures, but makes it much more difficult to throw light ones. Ultra-light rods have the opposite qualities, as you would expect. They are better at casting light lures and make catching smaller fish more enjoyable for the angler (Catching a sunfish with an extra-heavy rod feels like fishing with a pool cue. Catching one with an ultralight allows one to feel the fight).

A rod's action describes where the rod bends when pressure is applied to it. Rods with a faster action bend closer to their tip than rods with a slower one. There are reasons why you would want one as opposed to the other (generally, thinner hooks do better with slower action, as the rod will absorb more shock and the hook is less likely to pull from the fish), but to be frank, it doesn't matter as much when targeting smaller fish with children.

It's worth noting that neither power nor action are standardized measurements across the industry. One company's medium-heavy rating might be another company's medium rating, so try and shop for your first few rods in the store so you can see the difference and pick a good one for your kids.

Your child's age, size, and ability are going to directly influence what type of rod you purchase for them. When dealing with children 2-4 years old, you'll want to find a shorter rod in the 4 – 5' range, as that will be easier for them to manage. Such rods will likely have an ultra-light power rating which is perfect for panfish and works well enough for small bass. Ultralight rods mean that even small fish will put a pretty good bend in such a rod, and a decently sized fish may just bend it straight over for your child's first dance with a "big one!"

At about 5 or 6 years, it's possible that your kids will be able to cast a bit better and handle a bit larger rod in the 6' to 6'6" range. While they're still just a little tyke, by this age, they'll likely be able to handle lures like spinnerbaits well enough which will allow them to target larger species like pickerel, northern pike, and bass. An ultralight rod is not the best tool for this job. Instead, you'll want at least a rod rated as medium power, or even medium-heavy.

Once your kid is 8 to 10 years old, and assuming they've been at this for a while, they can handle anything in your rod box so long as it's light enough. With that said, they can still be a little too young to appreciate the value of a dollar, so you might want to hold off on buying them that $400 combo.

If you're looking to pick up a decent setup for an older child, I'd recommend looking for a medium-heavy rod in the 6'6" to 7' size range. Even though medium-heavy would suggest that it's not quite "in the middle" this is probably the most versatile setup you can purchase, so even if they already have one, they'll find use for another. It's ideal for plastic worms and spinnerbaits, can handle crankbaits or other treble hooks reasonably well, and do a decent job of handling plastic frogs or other lures designed to catch fish in deep cover. Depending on the brand, these rods can be a bit heavy to hold so you might want to look for one of a bit higher quality (and therefore lower weight). When purchasing quality for young anglers, a solid warranty or service plan is a must.

Don't be afraid to purchase a rod used to save some money. While you do need to do your due diligence to inspect the rod or photos, this can be a great way to get into some higher-quality setups for your family. Many of the elite, expensive brands have warranties that transfer to second owners. There's usually a deductible or fee of some sort. Knowing what that is ahead of time can help you figure out what price you need to purchase a used rod to break even in the worst-case scenario that it arrives damaged, or your kid immediately breaks it. For example, if a rod retails new for $200 and the manufacturer offers a no questions asked replacement warranty with a $75 deductible/fee, you can safely bid or offer up to $125 without putting yourself at risk. In the best-case scenario, you get a great rod for a fraction of the price, but even if things don't work out, you're simply paying MSRP. Most of my rods were purchased used putting this theory to the test. It's a great way to build up your inventory without breaking the bank. If you're interested in learning more about buying used fishing rods, I go into this topic at length on my blog, https://fishingfather.com/how-to-buy-used-fishing-rods-with-confidence/.

When choosing a rod, bear in mind that there are diminishing returns as you move up the price range. While there can be a huge difference between a $50 rod and a $150 rod, there is much less of a difference between a $150 rod and a $450 rod. As with most things in life, there is a balance. While you probably won't spend anywhere near this on a rod for a six-year-old, your kids are going to grow up eventually and they will be very susceptible to advertisements, so the law of diminishing returns is a concept worth teaching them early before they fall into debt.

Fishing Reels
Choosing a dependable, lightweight fishing reel that fits your child's hand can make a big difference to their enjoyment level out on the water. There are four main types of reels that you can put onto a rod: fly, spincast, baitcast, and spinning.

Fly reels should only go onto fly rods which are used for fly fishing, and I don't think many people are crazy enough to try to teach a toddler how to do that, so we won't get into those here. If you can get a two-year-old to fly fish, my hat's off to you, but it's beyond the scope of this book.

Spincast reels have been discussed a few times already and I've made no secret that I don't prefer them, but I don't want to stop you from using them if you value their simplicity. Not many companies make spincast reels so your options are going to be somewhat limited. Just make sure you find one small enough that your kid can comfortably hold. As stated earlier, buy a reel that is meant to catch fish rather than a young child's attention.

Baitcasting reels are, once again, not for children and I truly hope that by this point you've noticed how thickly I'm laying it on that you shouldn't run out and purchase one for them. I keep bringing them up though knowing that at least one of you will try it anyway. If you insist on being that guy, at least pony up enough cash to get a high-quality model that has several braking systems that can minimize backlashes. I would wager that inexpensive baitcasting reels are the number one reason people give up on baitcasting reels. You really don't want to skimp here and get the least expensive model as they can be significantly harder to use successfully. Save yourself some headaches and look for a reel in the $100-$150 range that has some bells and whistles. It's one of the few places in this book where I'll tell you that spending a large amount of money up front is worth it.

Spinning reels are my preferred choice for working with kids. All but the smallest children should be able to handle these without much issue, as even toddlers are surprisingly adaptable and capable of figuring them out. Most manufacturers offer a range of sizes and the trick is to try and match the size and weight of the reel to the rod you're using to have it balance well.

Sizes start at 1000 or 10 and go up as high as 30,000 or 300. The larger the number, the larger the spool and the greater the line capacity. A 2000 size reel is usually a pretty good match with a shorter rod. You could go to a 1000 but then its line capacity is going to be limited to 2 to 4lb test which can be challenging to use with toddlers without many breakoffs. I try not to go below 6lb test as I fish in areas where larger fish are plentiful.

It's not as important to purchase a high-quality spinning reel as it's with baitcasters, as there is no need for fancy braking systems just to cast the lure. I wouldn't recommend spending much money on your children's first few spinning reels at all, as it's probable that they'll be dropped in the dirt frequently. As spinning reels are open to the world, this can cause some problems. Dirt and precision equipment generally don't mix, and unless you invest some time on the internet learning how to disassemble, clean, and reassemble your reels, you could find them breaking down quickly and in need of replacement.

I'm not as comfortable purchasing used reels as I am with rods. There's just so much that can go wrong, and much of the damage or neglect is going to be internal and completely hidden from view if purchasing via an internet auction. For starters, it takes a bit of work and maintenance to keep reels performing indefinitely and you can't count on someone else having done that. Further, it's impossible to know from a photo online if a person used improper form and damaged the reel (such as by closing the bail of a spinning rod by reeling instead of flipping it shut manually).

I've been burned a few times buying used reels, so I'd recommend buying new. There are several good reels that can be had in the $40-$50 range. If you have one of the major tackle retailers near you, they tend to have a reel section with display models you can play with to see how much they weigh and how smoothly they operate. Go try a few out and see what one works best for you. When trying to match a reel to a rod to make your own combo, don't be afraid to take one out of the package and put it on a rod to see how the two balance together and feel to your kids—this is common practice in these stores.

Fishing Line

While there are several types of fishing line, I would strongly recommend that you stick to monofilament while teaching your kids to fish. I find it to be a safer option than braid, and easier to deal with than fluorocarbon. It's also the least expensive of the three by far, and you'll be going through plenty of line while your kids are discovering all the different ways to cause a tangle or snag a tree.

Fishing line comes in different pound tests for strength, and as the line's strength increases, so does the line's diameter, which means that you can't place as much line on your spool. 6lb test is a good starting place for most applications. It's strong enough that it can handle most of the fish your child is likely to catch, but also weak enough that it can easily be snapped if necessary when that spinnerbait is 30 feet high in a tree.

Terminal Tackle - Hooks

Most tackle shops devote a large section of their walls to nothing but hooks. There is a ridiculous amount of choice out there but as with other terminal tackle, we can cut that down tremendously if you're just trying to take your kids out fishing. Even so, you'll want a few different types in your arsenal: hooks designed for panfish, hooks designed for drop shots, hooks designed for using plastic worms in a "wacky rig," and circle hooks.

Panfish hooks are small and thin with a long shank. They are often called "baitholder hooks" and have a few small barbs on the shank as well as the point, designed to keep squiggly worms firmly attached.

While they come in many sizes, you can find a hook that will work well with the eyeball test. When you're looking through the terminal tackle aisle, try to find a hook that looks like it could fit into a bluegill's mouth, but can still hold a worm. The shank should be long so that it can be expected to protrude from the fish's mouth for ease of removal. Such hooks are very inexpensive, so pick up several different packs as you'll be losing many of them to trees and other snags.

Bear in mind that you can tie a dropshot with any kind of hook, so if you want to minimize your initial investment, stick to the panfish hooks and call it a day.

If you're seeking a "dedicated" drop shot hook, they are also called "mosquito hooks." They almost look like little tear drops and come in a variety of sizes. Again, you want to use the old eyeball test and a little common sense to find one small enough to fit in a panfish mouth, but you also need one large enough where your bait (either a live minnow or an imitation) can be hooked through the mouth and be secured against the bend of the hook. A size 2 is usually pretty good for panfish applications.

"Wacky Rig" worm hooks look very similar to drop shot hooks but have a wider gap to accommodate wider plastics. These are the hooks you're going to use to try and catch larger fish like bass, so it's not important to consider ones that will fit in a panfish's mouth. Often, the plastic worm you'll thread on these hooks is the same size as a panfish in the first place!

Circle hooks are designed with for fishing with live bait, as it's more likely to be deeply swallowed. Their hook point is curved in towards the bend of the hook with the idea being that it's unlikely to hook a fish deep in its belly. You don't "set" a circle hook with a jerk of the rod – you simply reel it in. If the fish's mouth is pointed away from you when you do this (as it will tend to be when the fish detects your pressure), the hook will rotate and catch against the corner of the fish's mouth for easy removal. Circle hooks are widely viewed as more humane and a better option for catch and release fishing for this reason. They're a must when fishing for catfish or bullhead.

As your child's skills develop, you can explore other hook types, but those described above are what you need to stock to give them the best chance of fast action. Fishing with small children is all about quantity over an adult's perception of "quality."

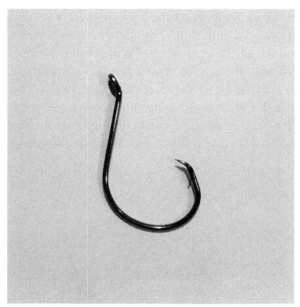

The point of a circle hook curves inward and is designed to catch the corner of a fish's mouth when reeled in. Don't try setting the hook by jerking the rod, as that will pull the hook away without snagging the fish.

Terminal Tackle – Weights

Certain presentations such as drop shots require weights to work effectively. As with the litany of other fishing products to buy, these too come in all shapes and sizes and it can get very confusing very fast. Don't worry too much about what the shape of the weight is – they all have the same basic purpose – to drag your lure or bait down quickly and keep it at or near the bottom. Some shapes are designed to travel over rocks without snagging while others are meant to glide through weeds, but most can pass just fine in different roles, and none are guaranteed not to snag, anyway.

Try to match the size of the weight to the weather conditions. The windier and wavier it is out there, the heavier the weight you're going to need to keep your rig where you want it. On the other hand, heavier weights have the drawback of potentially tipping off the fish to danger before they have a chance to become hooked. You should therefore try to use the smallest weight possible for the weather conditions.

Many manufacturers offer dedicated drop shot weights. These arc designed to break away when they get snagged, so you only lose your weight and not your entire rig. They do this by crimping the "eye" that you would normally tie your line to. What you're meant to do is thread your line through the eye, then tie a simple knot in the line itself a bit beyond the eye. Don't tie the knot on the eye itself. You then slip the line up through the crimped section of the eye. The knot you tied in the line will hold it against the crimp during normal circumstances but will also be the weakest section and will fail first if you get snagged.

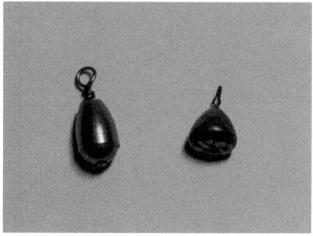

Specially designed drop shot weights (right) have a crimped eye designed for snugging line in, rather than needing to tie a knot, as with traditional weights (left).

Bait

You're going to need to present some sort of enticement, or bait, to a fish in order to catch it. You can use live bait, such as nightcrawlers, or artificial lures designed to mimic living food. Which type you should choose depends on what you're trying to accomplish. Live bait is better when fishing with young children, or when conditions are tough. Artificial lures can be better if you're able to move around to "power fish," (such as with teenagers). Further, artificial lures are required in many fishing tournaments, so if your children are interested in competitive fishing, they need to learn how to use them.

If you're using bait, please consider using circle hooks described above as fish tend to swallow these offerings and can be badly hurt or killed if you can't quickly remove the hook without much agitation.

Types of Bait
You can put just about any type of prey or food substance on the end of your hook that you're comfortable with and the law allows for, but the most common are worms, minnows, corn, bread, chicken liver, leaches and other critters.

Worms
The classic nightcrawler is probably the bait everyone started with (it certainly was for me, and for my kids). For some reason, fish love worms, and are quick to eat them.

Worms make a great bait to bring along with the kids because they'll attract every fish in the lake. When you're going for quantity, it's hard to beat them.

One great thing about worms is that you probably have them right in your yard and garden. Kids love digging for them and it can be a fun part of the fishing trip just going and gathering their own bait. With that said, they are worth buying at the store if you can't find big, plump, juicy ones on your own.

Minnows
Minnows are little bait fish that you can purchase by the dozen from many tackle shops. They come in a range of species and sizes and make good bait. They aren't as hardy as worms and tend to be "big fish bait" though they will catch smaller species too, assuming the smaller fish can fit the minnow in their mouth.

Some people will tell you to go catch your own minnows, but I would urge you to check local regulations before you do this, and only use fish from the same waterway you intend to fish. There have been some issues over the years with certain invasive species being introduced to a lake or river this way.

Some places, like Lake Champlain, regulate which species of minnows can be used, and insist on proof of purchase to confirm that they were sourced appropriately. There are hefty fines for those caught without a receipt.

The bottom line is you can get in a world of trouble if you're not careful using minnows, so if you intend to use your own, I would recommend calling your local game warden or ask the owner of your local tackle shop for insight into the laws of the waters you intend to fish to ensure that you are being lawful.

Corn

I used to have a lot of fun as a kid at a local pond fishing for sunfish with corn. Two or three little kernels seemed to be all I needed to get fish to bite on the right day (though on others, they'd just stare perplexed at the offering).

If you don't have access to nightcrawlers, or simply don't want to use them, corn can work well as a substitute. Just make sure that you check your local regulations as certain places consider it littering, or "feeding the animals" which is banned in many waters.

Bread

Bread can work very well for bluegill and sunfish. What you do is take some and ball it up so that you can pierce it with a hook. As the water softens the bread, you're going to need to replace it as it will eventually fall off.

As with corn, you should check your local regulations because there is a chance that this could be considered littering, and some places don't want you feeding the ducks bread, so you shouldn't be caught with a loaf.

Chicken Liver

While disgusting, chicken liver works great for catfish, bullhead, bowfin, and other exotic species. It is very hard to keep on the hook, but if you manage to, it's hard to beat. If you present this in an area where these large fish can find it, they'll eat it.

It smells horrific and makes a terrible mess, however, so I wouldn't recommend using it from a brand-new boat if you're partial to how the carpet looks and smells. It also attracts flies and other insects quickly and so it isn't always the most pleasant way to fish.

If you're having a hard time keeping it on your hook, you can use some old cut up cheesecloth or panty hose to make a little pouch. Really, any fabric that is porous would work – the idea is that you want the scent to disperse.

Leeches and Other Critters

There are a host of other types of bait. Basically, anything that a fish would normally eat can be attached to hook and used to entice a bite. Walleye anglers love leaches, many trophy bluegill hunters swear by crickets, and countless catfish have been caught with cut up bluegill.

You can use just about anything, but I would, once again, urge you to check your local regulations just to make sure you're fully compliant with the law. Further, try to be humane. While I won't pass judgement on your decision to use certain types of bait where legal, I would implore you to be a decent person when you use it. If you're going to cut up a bluegill for catfish, please kill the bluegill first with a good strike to its head.

When to Use Bait

I would recommend using bait of some sort when it's legal and you absolutely need to catch a fish, such as when fishing with kids. Once upon a time, I envisioned teaching my son how to fish without ever using bait, as I'm not totally comfortable with the morality of it, but this didn't last very long as my pragmatism took over.

I owed it to him to help him learn how to fish and to do that I had to make sure he had fun his first few times out. You do that by putting fish on the hook, not by insisting on artificial only fishing techniques.

Bait is also great for a more leisurely fishing approach. It can be very relaxing to sit on the bank with a rod and enjoy the sunset while waiting for a catfish to swim by, or to play catch with your kids while a few rods rest on a forked stick waiting for a bluegill.

With all that said, fishing is only going to be as good as the fishing spot. It's impossible to catch a fish that isn't there, after all. I find that a lot of the fishermen who are using bait don't seem to catch many fish and this is because they tend to wait for the fish to find them rather than going out in search of them. If you're in the wrong spot, fishing with bait can be exceptionally boring.

When to Use Artificial Lures

Use an artificial lure when you don't have bait available, or any time that you want to get better at fishing, because every time you cast one out you're practicing with it and building experience that you can apply later (especially if you decide to fish tournaments someday).

You may also find that artificial lures are easier to use around heavy weeds and other cover, mostly because live bait tends to leave the hook exposed and will foul easily in such conditions. There are certain artificial lures and ways to rig them that are ideally suited for fishing in slop or laydowns and will come through without much issue.

Artificial lures are also very useful when you want to cover a lot of water by "power fishing" and searching for the active fish in an area. While there's nothing that says you can't also power fish with live bait, it probably won't hold up to repeated casting as well and you may find it often flies off the hook. Also, most live bait is fished slowly and with power fishing you really want to cover a lot of water quickly.

Finally, you should use artificial lures if you are in a bass fishing tournament because chances are if you don't, you're in violation of the tournament rules!

Hybrid Lures vs. Live Bait

There is a third option. Some manufacturers have designed plastic lures that mimic the scent, shape, and taste of baitfish and other critters. While technically artificial lures and not live bait, they almost come across as a "hybrid." They tend to be very supple lures with great action and come doused in scent and attractant. These make them my all-time favorite drop shot lures.

These products are a great alternative if you have moral or philosophical objections to using live bait while fishing, but still want your kids to have a good time. They also tend to produce less mess than live bait (though, given how much scent they are doused in, they will still leave some mess if you aren't careful).

One thing I don't like about these products is that it's difficult to keep them fresh as they dry out quickly when their bag is opened. Some manufacturers offer jars of such lures which seem to work better as the lure remains in liquid until you need it.

If you buy the jars, make sure you keep them out of the sun as the liquid heats up quickly and tends to make the lures even softer and more likely to pull from the hook.

Three Great Artificial Lures for Using with Kids

While the only tackle you really "need" is the gear required to rig a drop shot, there are some other lures that work well for kids and are worthy of consideration. These lures work well, and children can easily handle them. They are also less likely to injure a novice angler (or the patient adult standing precariously nearby). They are the spinnerbait, roundhead jig, and plastic worm.

Spinnerbaits

The spinnerbait is my go-to lure for fishing with anyone who is both new to fishing, but capable of casting out a substantial distance. It is a simple lure to fish, as all you must do is cast it out and reel it in. The spinnerbaits flashing blades and pulsating skirt will be more than an active fish can resist. Varying the speed of your retrieve or giving it a little pop now and then will help, but you're perfectly likely to catch something just by reeling it in as well.

Spinnerbaits are one of the safer lures for kids to use because they feature a single, large hook that requires more force to pierce skin than a narrow treble hook. Further, this hook is protected somewhat by a bent wire frame in front of it, so even if a cast is a little errant, it's unlikely that the hook will do much damage.

Spinnerbaits are very versatile as you can fish them near all sorts of cover without much risk of losing them. Their bent wire frame deflects most obstacles and protects the hook. So as long as you keep the lure in constant motion (thus, not allowing it to drop at an angle and catch the hook on a tree branch), it will move through most hard cover, like laydowns and rocks, easily. They can slip through weeds as well, though they will be fouled by heavy vegetation.

They come in a variety of shapes, colors, and sizes, all designed for specialized applications, but a white 3/8 oz spinnerbait will work well for kids in most situations and would be a good place to start.

As you go through the tackle shop, you'll notice that the blades on the spinnerbait have different shapes. The two most popular ones are called "willow leaf blades" and "Colorado blades." Willow leaf blades are long and thin. They are designed to flash and visually attract fish. Colorado blades are wider and more circular. They attract fish by vibrating and disturbing the water. Both work well, but if you're fishing clearer water during the day where fish can see further, it makes sense to concentrate on willow leaf blades. If you're planning on fishing murky water, or fishing during low light conditions, sometimes Colorado blades are better.

Willow leaf (top) and Colorado (bottom) blades each have different applications.

A spinnerbait will catch any fish in the lake that can fit it in its mouth, but these lures work best or chain pickerel, northern pike, and bass. I've caught very large catfish and bowfin on them as well, though this is rarer.

You'll increase your chances of catching fish with spinnerbaits if you are moving constantly. This is will allow you to cover a lot of water and to aggressively search for active fish. This is easy to do from a boat – simply drift along and cast as many times and in as many directions as you can while you go. If you're on shore, you'll get some exercise.

I like to keep spinnerbaits moving through the water, but the exact speed depends on the situation. In general, I've had better luck reeling them in fast than slow. If I'm "slow rolling" a spinnerbait, it usually means that the conditions are such that I'd probably be better off just using a plastic worm or drop shot.

A spinnerbait will sink if it's not reeled in, and sometimes a fish will hit it while it's dropping, but it would be unusual for a fish to pick it up if you left it on the bottom. With that said, it's sometimes a good idea to let it sink for a few seconds to target deeper fish. Once you start your retrieve, it will start climbing upwards, so this is a technique better used with a long cast.

Spinnerbaits are also great lures for trolling for chain pickerel, which can be a wonderful way to use them when you're with smaller children who can't cast very well just yet. Just get your boat up to speed with a trolling motor or kicker, cast the lure out as far as you can behind you, let out a bit of extra line, and hold on. You'll need to ensure your lure doesn't foul with weeds, but if it stays clean you can cover a lot of water this way and present an enticing target to numerous fish quickly. Trolling is a great way to use these lures with smaller children.

I break out my spinnerbaits once the water temperature reaches about 60° and I don't put them down again until ice forms on the lake. I find them to be very ineffective in cold water *except* in the fall when the cooling temperatures raise an alarm in fish warning that winter is coming. The cooling temperatures and shorter days often cause fish to feed voraciously and attack anything they can.

Because spinnerbaits are fairly weedless, I like to find weedy bays that have enough clear water in-between the weed stems or above the canopy to let my spinnerbait move through the water without fouling too often, and I tend to reel them in quickly in these areas. They make for very good lures to cast in larger pockets or alleyways between weeds as this puts them in the strike zone for a considerable time.

I've had a lot of success with spinnerbaits at dawn, but my personal experience is they've been less useful at dusk. This might just be a result of my favoring willow leaf styles that rely on reflecting the sun's glare to shine brilliantly, however, but I just think that fish have trouble adjusting to a fast-moving target right while the sun is setting.

There are plenty of people that throw them later at night, but this is after the fish have had a chance to adjust, and these folks are usually throwing Colorado blades as well.

A spinnerbait was one of the first lures my father handed to me when I was a kid, and I'd argue they should be one of the first lures you hand to your child as well. The only drawback over plastic worms is that your kid must be good at casting before they use spinnerbaits, since these are meant to cast and retrieve repeatedly.

Roundhead Jigs

Roundhead jigs don't get as much love throughout the entire country as they do in the Northeast, but many anglers here have several in their tackle box. I can tell you from experience that they're great lures for kids as they were one of the mainstays of my own childhood.

Although their hook is generally a thin wire, it's a single hook and so it isn't as dangerous as a treble hook. You also might consider bending the barb down or filing it off to make the lure barbless to further minimize risk of injury.

These lures work great for bass and panfish but leave something to be desired for northern pike and pickerel as they are small lures that have no built-in protection from sharp teeth. Attempting to use a wire leader would kill their action and I don't recommend it. They are inexpensive enough that you should just accept losing a few.

They can be rigged in several different ways, from the marabou style in the picture below, to tipped with small artificial grubs or even live minnows.

The marabou jig: a mainstay of northern waters.

Roundhead jigs are easy for kids to cast and they work in a variety of retrieves, which is great for kids who haven't yet mastered taking directions! Kids can find success regardless of how they're fishing them, just so long as they keep them moving. They can cast them out and bounce them back in, do a straight retrieve, lift the rod and let it fall back down in place, or a combination of all three.

Another great quality about these jigs is that they will catch just as many panfish as bass, especially if you use a smaller size. A 1/8 oz or lower can easily catch yellow and white perch as well as crappie and bluegill, while still being attractive towards nearby lurking bass. This makes them a great lure for children, as they can usually get bit easily. If you tip these lures with worms, that increases considerably, as one would expect.

If you were tipping the jig with a minnow, you might even consider fishing one underneath of a bobber. The jig head would provide enough weight that the minnow wouldn't go very far, and the bobber would keep the presentation up where fish can see it and away from the bottom where it could be snagged.

I like to fish a roundhead jig during the spring, as they're awesome lures for fishing the rip-rap shores that smallmouth often spawn on. When I was little, Dad used to just drift along entire shorelines with this type of habitat, and we'd throw marabou jigs repeatedly.

These aren't going to work as well in weedy flats, but they could work fine on the weed *edge*. This is not a weedless design and picking slime off marabou feathers is a pain you want to avoid, but you do need to cast where the fish are, and the fish are near cover.

These kinds of jigs also get some play from ice fishermen during the winter months. Marabou feathers give a lot of action to a lure that is otherwise standing still, which can be a good combination in frigid conditions.

Depending on where you live, you may not have heard of these lures, but that also means the fish probably haven't seen them, either. It never hurts to show a fish a new trick – they often fall for them.

Plastic Worms

It seems like every article I've ever read about teaching kids how to fish suggests that parents buy some plastic worms. I agree wholeheartedly. It's hard to fish these lures wrong, and I've had plenty of days where they beat everything else in the boat. It is not at all uncommon for this to be a "one cast, one fish" lure under the right conditions.

While you can rig plastic worms dozens of different ways, I usually rig mine "wacky rigged." It has several advantages when fishing with kids. The main strength is that unlike a Texas rig, the hook is exposed, so it doesn't require much of a hookset. This is a big plus when fishing with children who can forget to set the hook and tend to just reel in when they feel a bite.

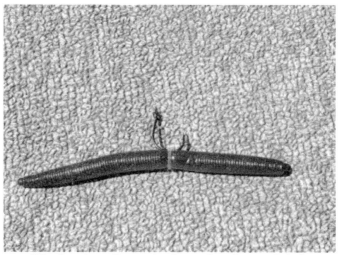

The "wacky rig" is perfect for catching bass with kids.

The first time I saw a wacky rig, I thought it looked like something a child came up with – you just stick a hook right in the middle of the worm and call it a day. Well, I'm not sure on the history exactly, but if a kid did think of it or inspire it, then that kid was on to something, because this is a phenomenal presentation for youngsters.

I suppose you could use any worm on a wacky rig, but the one that is ubiquitous with the technique is known as a stick bait. These worms tend to look like sticks (hence the name). They are soft and supple and loaded with salt which gives them great action and attraction.

As you can see in the photo above, I have one wacky rigged. You might notice that there is a clear plastic band in the middle of the worm, that I have the hook looped on. This is called a wacky-worm o-ring, and you really want to buy them. Plastic worms are so soft that they tear off the hook easily if you just hook them directly. Attaching them via the o-ring as shown above will allow you to get much more use out of them, which is important because they are expensive and you don't want to see them fly off the hook on your fifth cast.

Plastic worms will catch most fish that are large enough to fit them in their mouth, but the main species you'll catch are largemouth bass. I've also caught more than my fair share of chain pickerel, northern pike, and even a few bowfin, but you do run a strong risk that these toothy predators will cut through your line.

It's possible for a plastic worm to catch large bluegills and sunfish too, but you're more likely to just feel them nibbling away as the lure tends to be much larger than their mouths. This isn't the end of the world – at least you know there are fish around. Just change your tactics to the dropshot and go catch them!

These are great lures for kids because all they need to do is cast it out, and let it sink. After the worm, lift the rod tip up to raise it and then allow the worm to sink again. Most strikes will come on the fall. Occasionally, I'll raise my rod tip less high and do this 3-4 times in rapid succession. These little "taps" make the worm scurry across the bottom towards me. Once I've made the taps, I reel in the slack.

At other times I will simply allow the lure to sit still on the bottom and leave it there for some time. This works especially well in situations where I suspect a bass is lurking nearby, such as near a bed during the spawn, or under a particularly shady boat dock.

You can use wacky-rigged worms all year long, but they are absolute dynamite during the spawn. Casting near bass beds will quickly produce results, and usually all you need to do to get a limit is to find a good spawning bay and start probing likely areas. If you're in a healthy ecosystem that hasn't been overly pressured, it won't be long before you get bit.

I have better luck with wacky-rigged plastic worms when it isn't that windy. The one drawback of the lure is that it's a technique where you really need to be able to feel the fish bite and observe your line moving sideways as a fish swims off with it. Both are tough to feel or see in high winds.

This isn't usually a problem, because I'm usually casting these lures in shallow bays that tend to be protected somewhat from the wind. I like to try and cast in little pockets of clear water between weeds, especially around creek mouths, points, or other structure that fish will relate to.

That can be a little tough for smaller kids, but once they get to be about six or seven, they are able to pinpoint their casts better and this technique should really shine.

In the meanwhile, this is a good presentation for you to fish and then hand your kid the rod, as you're normally hooking the fish a few feet away from cover (as opposed to frogs, where you're fishing in the thick of it). You just need to keep a high bend in your rod while your child is scrambling over, and then they can take command and reel it in.

Other Useful Items

The premise of this chapter was to break things down to six items you absolutely needed, which I've done. Below, I'll describe a few more items that aren't critical, but can come in handy.

Helpful Tools

You'll save yourself many headaches if you bring a few key tools along with you on any trip. The good news is you probably have these lying around your house.

A must-have are needle nose plyers for safely removing hooks, as they give you leverage and allow you to reach deeper into mouths than you could (or would want to) with your hands. If you catch something with teeth, you'll be glad you brought these along. A good pair of scissors is also useful, especially if you're fishing with braid, as it's difficult to cut with plyers. Finally, a small set of bolt cutters is imperative for cutting through hooks that are embedded where they shouldn't be.

While you probably won't have mouth spreaders lying around, you might want to pick up a pair if you're targeting northern pike and pickerel as they are handy for keeping toothy grins wide open so you can safely take out the hook.

Tackle Box

Eventually, you're going to want some way to keep and organize your tackle. Years ago, the most common method was a hard-plastic tackle box. Though these are still manufactured, they've fallen out of favor in recent years. These days, most anglers are using soft-sided tackle bags that resemble luggage and fill those tackle bags with several clear plastic containers. The main advantage here is that the containers can be swapped in and out as necessary. For example, if you live in the north, you probably wouldn't bother with a box full of plastic frogs in March—you'd want to bring your jerkbaits and jigs instead. If you were using an old tackle box, that would mean you'd need to go in and remove each lure individually. With the bag system, you just swap out the clear plastic "frog" container for another containing jerkbaits.

Some of these tackle bags are backpacks, and a few of them even have a cooler section built in. If you're fishing from shore and expect to do much walking, these are probably your best bet. You want something small enough that it won't cause you back pain but also large enough that you can fit a bunch of snacks, drinks, spare clothes, and a game or two to keep the little ones occupied if the fish aren't quite ready to bite.

Even though the traditional tackle box has fallen out of favor, there's still a place for it – your kids. Despite your hard work and best intentions, the fish won't always cooperate. Kids enjoy playing with tackle boxes and so long as you are thoughtful about what you put in them, (no treble hooks and only soft plastics that don't have health warnings) the tackle box can be a good source of amusement while waiting for a bite.

Terminal Tackle – Snaps and Swivels

The phrase "terminal tackle" basically refers to any object you're going to tie onto your line that isn't a lure. There are a ton of different types that all have their own application, but for the purposes of taking a kid out, you only need to know about snaps and swivels.

Snaps are little metal clasps that are meant to be tied to your line and then attached to your lure of choice. They allow you to change lures much quicker because you don't have to tie a new knot every time you change a lure – you just unclasp the snap, slide the old lure off, and slide the new lure on. Their drawback is that they add weight to the front of the lure which can alter or kill its action. If you're going to a use a snap, try and use the smallest one that you can for this reason.

Swivels are objects with two eyes that are connected to a pivoting joint that can rotate 360 degrees. One eye is tied to the main line, and the other is usually tied to a leader. Some swivels feature three eyes, each going in a different direction. They are meant to attach two tag lines to the main line, often so that one can have a hook attached, and the other can have a sinker. Swivels eliminate line twist because their pivoting joint swings freely, meaning that the main line doesn't have to twist around itself as lures move through the water.

When one of the swivel's eyes is attached to a snap, the terminal tackle is called a "snap swivel." These combine the benefits of snaps (easy lure changes) and swivels (eliminated line twist) but at the cost of even more weight on the lure, which can potentially kill its action. As with snaps, you'll want to choose the smallest one you can get away with depending on the size of fish you're seeking (remember, snaps and snap swivels are another thing that can fail).

Because they eliminate the need to tie a new knot with every lure change, snaps and snap swivels are great tools for allowing children some independence as they'll be better able to experiment with different lures in different situations. They're not as necessary for younger kids who aren't trusted to touch hooks and therefore are going to use what you tell them to use when you tell them to use it.

Odds & Ends

While snaps, hooks, and weights are the main terminal tackle that you need, you should also find room for plastic o-rings, and maybe a few bobbers.

O-Rings are must-haves for wacky-rigging worms as they make the presentation affordable. Wacky rig worms are very soft which gives them an enticing action, but also makes them very prone to ripping from the hook on the cast, or after a bite. O-Rings will let you use the same worm longer. They are little rubber circles that you slide up to the middle of your plastic worm. You then secure your hook to this ring rather than hooking through the worm itself. This significantly increases the lifespan of these lures, which is important for soft plastics that can run close to $8 for a pack of 10.

It can be challenging to put an o-ring onto a plastic worm by hand, as they don't all fit very well. Rolling it up will tend to scar the worm and risk tearing it to pieces. There is a tool you can buy which has you stick the worm into a cylinder and then slide the o-ring over the same cylinder and onto the worm. This works great, but if you'd like to save $5 you can use a tool you already have – your needle nose pliers. Simply thread the o-ring onto the pliers and then open them up wide enough to accommodate the worm. Then, relax the pliers and slide the o-ring onto the worm as desired.

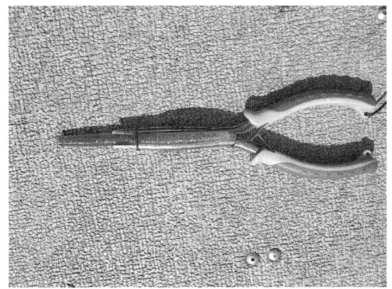

While you can purchase a specialty tool, your trusty needle nose pliers work just fine for threading an O-Ring onto a plastic worm.

Even if you're brand new to fishing, you probably have seen a bobber before – it's just a piece of foam or plastic designed to indicate a fish strike and keep bait up above weeds. They come in different shapes and sizes for different presentations, but generally speaking I try to keep them as small as possible as I don't like fish to realize something is wrong, and my theory is that the pressure from a bobber going under is a good hint to them that they're in trouble.

To be perfectly candid, I'm not that big of a fan of bobbers. In fact, I'd go so far as to say they'll bore your children right out of this sport.

I know I'm going to get flak for that statement as I'm sure there are plenty of people out there who have successfully taught their kids how to fish by using bobbers. Perhaps you're one of them. Well, steady that pitchfork for a moment.

I don't like bobbers because it's my belief that a huge percentage of parents who don't really know how to fish, but want to try it with their kids, rig up a bobber, kind of throw it out there, and just hope for the best–but the best never comes. I think that's a recipe for disaster.

Most beginners fishing with a bobber are hedging their bets that a fish will be in the area, or swim by, rather than going out and actively finding them. Again, if you are in a good spot, then this doesn't matter. But if you aren't, you're inhibiting your ability to go out and find where the fish are holding so they can be caught more frequently.

Bobbers seem to go hand in hand with lawn chairs, which kids are terrible at sitting in for any extended period. I think you're far better off with a more active technique (such as a drop shot), walking around the pond, making many casts, and trying to locate active fish. This will keep your kids far more engaged and enthused than sitting around, waiting for a bobber to plunge.

I'm not arguing against having bobbers, as they have their time and place. I'm merely arguing that bobbers aren't very conducive to keeping your children's attention. I know I said that fishing teaches kids patience, but that's a relative term. It might gain you about twelve seconds lead time with a four-year-old.

6 – FRESHWATER GAMEFISH

It stands to reason that if you're going fishing you might as well know a thing or two about the species you're trying to catch. This book won't cover them all as it exclusively deals with freshwater gamefish of North America, and specifically those that can be found in lakes and ponds. If you're after trout or other major river species, I'm sorry to disappoint. With that said, many of the species described below are found in rivers too.

I also have no intention of covering every single gamefish that you might find in a lake or pond. Instead, I will describe the more common ones that you might target with your children. Not all of these species are going to be in your backyard, but chances are you'll have more than a few of them. I'll list them in order of what I would consider the simplest to catch with children, with the easiest fish first.

Panfish

This is a large category of fish that considers just about anything small enough to fit inside of a pan, hence the name. Typically, it comprises of sunfish, bluegills, yellow perch, white perch, rock bass, and crappie.

These are ideal first fish to target with children because they are widespread, numerous, eager to bite, and relatively stupid (at least in their younger, smaller years). They can often be spotted in the shallows and spend a good portion of their life close enough to shore to be caught without a boat. They also put up a fun fight on ultralight rods, to the delight of your kids. All in all, panfish make outstanding targets.

Nightcrawlers are a great bait for panfish, but you'll get more use out of them if you pinch off a section of worm and just place it on the tip of the hook. Even the tiniest morsel right on the point will work. If you put an entire worm on a hook, most of it will be stolen before you finally hook a fish. If you can't buy or find worms in your area, don't despair. Panfish will strike even the simplest of bait, so even canned corn or pinched bread will bring success.

Another presentation that works very well is a drop shot with a small minnow imitation. Panfish will hit minnows 2.5" and larger, but 2" and below make hook ups more likely. I favor natural colors whenever I can find them. Some will tell you that you need a bright color like chartreuse in stained water, but I fish the southern end of Lake Champlain frequently with its vast stretches of chocolate milk-colored water and don't find the bright ones work any better. Most of these minnows contain some sort of scent and I think that is doing more for the fish than the color, but your mileage may vary.

You can also try very small artificial lures. These are specifically labeled "Crappie" or "Panfish" lures and include small spinnerbaits and grubs. These too will work though some of them are difficult for younger children to cast effectively as they are very light.

The easiest time to catch panfish is around the bass spawn. This will vary depending on where you are from and has much to do with water temperature. When it reaches a range of 55° to 65° (anywhere from January in Florida to late June in Canada), bass will move into shallow bays to spawn, and armadas of panfish will follow them to rob their eggs.

These armadas are very hard to miss, especially if the sun is angled right to cast their shadows. You'll see a large school of fish concentrated within about a 5' circle. What they're doing is waiting for the bass to turn their back or get distracted so they can swoop in for an easy meal of eggs. You'll find they're also perfectly happy to eat a slowly falling worm.

Even if your water is too stained to see the panfish, there are different signs that they're present. The most obvious is a large pattern of splashes that will happen in the same general spot every few minutes. This means that a panfish got within range of mama or papa bass and the larger fish took a swipe at it. This causes the entire panfish school to scatter, jump, and make quite a fuss. If you notice a disturbance like this a few times in the same place, there is a bass bed with panfish nearby. The bass will usually get aggressive every 2-5 minutes, so you won't be waiting long (it can be quite convenient to watch for these while you're dealing with one of your kids' tangles).

My son and I have caught all sorts of panfish doing this, and some of them have been quite large. The most common types seem to be sunfish of one sort or another (mainly pumpkinseed and bluegill where we are from), but it isn't uncommon to find yellow perch raiding nests as well. As a nice bonus, you'll often eventually catch the bass as well.

Panfish conduct their own spawn shortly after the bass spawn concludes. Look for their nests when the water temperature approaches 70° or so. While you might not find a huge school over any one nest, there are more panfish than bass, ergo more panfish nests than bass nests—an area can hold quite a few. They'll be in the same general area and the fish will strike anything they perceive as a danger to their eggs. Being fish, and dense ones at that, they'll think a worm is such an intruder.

Fishing during the spawn raises ethical questions. So long as what you're doing is legal in the area, this question is between you and God, but I would put this out there: a fish cannot guard its nest when it's sitting in the livewell or frying pan. Some states, especially in the north, protect the spawning season of certain fish for this reason.

You should also bear in mind that fish are like any other creature in that those that are genetically predisposed to reach a greater size tend to have offspring that share this trait. If you want to catch large fish in the future, wouldn't you want those young to have the best chance of survival? Please consider practicing a selective harvest, and let the true giants swim back to guard their young.

Unfortunately, the spawn doesn't last forever, and you'll eventually need to find other places to catch fish. As spring transitions to summer, boat docks, rock formations and other areas with shade offer consistent action for little anglers. Panfish will also remain in the same bays where they spawned, holding to weed cover. They may, however, be a bit deeper than you found them in the spring. Their appetite will remain voracious and if you can find them, you'll be able to catch them. The most challenging part is finding places where your kid can accurately cast to them without immediately snagging weeds.

In creeks or rivers, look for areas where there is a pool of water a little deeper than elsewhere that also has something breaking up the current a bit. You'd be surprised how many fish even a small creek can hold.

I took my son out once to a local pond that is separated from a small feeder creek by a culvert. Depending on the time of year and flood stage, the current will either head towards the creek or into the pond. This process creates deep pools on either side of the culvert which attract fish as they're able to hide in the pools and ambush anything that gets swept their way.

At the time I took him, the water was so high in the pond that it was dumping into the creek. There were several laydowns (felled trees) at the mouth of the culvert, over the deeper pool. Fish were holding below this, and it was simply a matter of casting a worm out and letting it sink in the current. This provided constant action for several hours.

Even a creek this small can provide
constant panfish action!

Panfish are caught in large numbers throughout the winter by ice fishermen. Live bait is usually more productive, but it can get expensive given that little minnows usually won't hold up past a few bites. The same small artificial minnows that you would utilize on a drop shot can be used while ice fishing, and they'll often hold up for several fish.

Ice fishing is another time when chumming works very well, though you'll want to ensure that the practice is legal on your body of water. You probably won't be as mobile while ice fishing so anything you can do to bring the fish towards you is a good thing.

As seen, these small fish provide year-round action for small anglers and should be your first target when hitting the lake with children. You'll probably get some bigger bites from other fish while you're at it, and your trip will be successful if your kids get some bites early. You can try upgrading for size after that, and anything larger will be gravy.

Bullhead & Catfish

If your area allows multiple rods, it wouldn't be the worst idea in the world to have a spare bait soaking in the water trying to entice a bite from a bullhead or catfish while you actively fish with another rig. The ideal situation is that your kids are having a blast reeling in the smaller fish one by one when a few feet down the bank, your larger catfish rod bends over in two!

Fishing for bullhead and catfish can nicely compliment the panfish bite, especially when you are chumming an area. The same rabbit food that draws in bluegill will draw in giant channel cats and bullhead. Conveniently, an ideal bait for the larger fish is cut up panfish, so if a panfish swallows the hook and can't be saved, its death needn't be in vain.

You might catch a few bullheads on the same ultralight rigs that you're targeting panfish with as they too will swipe at cut up worms, but hooking a catfish on one of these would be a very challenging fight, especially with a thin wire panfish hook attached to such a small rod. It's very likely that the catfish will break off, but that's OK. Every fisherman, including your kids, needs their own story about the giant fish that got away.

If you're deliberately targeting catfish as a "bonus fish," then you'll want your second or third (where legal) rod to be substantially beefier and capable of handling a larger catfish. Down south, some species of catfish can weigh over 100lbs. Even in the north, channel cats can grow larger than 20lbs. You'll want at least a medium-heavy rod spooled with 17-20lb test monofilament. The good news is that it doesn't take a particularly sensitive or expensive rod to let bait soak on the water, you just need one strong enough to fight a large fish.

85

There are many choices for bait, but the biggest key is it should stink. Cut up bluegill or other small fish work very well, but if you would prefer not to kill one and cut it up in front of your children, there are other options. One is to go to your local bait shop and ask for some large, dead shiners. You can also use chicken liver that you can find at your local supermarket. This works great so long as you can keep it on the hook, but it's very messy, and you'll have flies everywhere. It's almost impossible not to get the blood and juice all over the place and if you're going to use it from a boat, make sure the boat isn't very nice.

Many people use worms for catfish, though they generally will put three or four mashed together on the hook instead of just one. This works fine if you can count on the bait being unmolested by panfish while you wait for your catfish to show up, but since we're looking at these fish as "bonus fish" in the middle of a panfish feeding frenzy, worms probably won't work that well for you.

Other natural baits include everything from muscles, leeches, frogs, to salamanders—just about anything plump and juicy will do the trick. These baits can be dead or alive, though the largest cats tend to favor the live ones. Ironically, this is a good reason to use dead bait—you want your kid to have a chance at catching a fish larger than your typical panfish—not be pulled into the water by one. A 5lb juvenile would do marvelously.

You can also find many man-made, processed baits on the market. These have a variety of names, but all could generally fall into the category of "stink bait" because they smell horrible. Most are doughs, paste, or slime. When you open the container, you will swear that some kid at the tackle shop slacked a bit and left them out in the sun for a few hours, but this is normal. These offerings do have the advantage of generally being resealable and therefore easy to transport or use over multiple days, but they also tend to catch smaller catfish (which, again, may be desirable with children).

Some of these baits are difficult to keep on the hook. Chicken liver is notorious for slipping off during the cast and flinging into the abyss, and most dip baits would quickly dissolve on a regular hook. Some options to keep chicken liver in place include wrapping it in some cut up pantyhose or cheesecloth – the smell can still escape but the bait is less likely to. For stink bait, they sell hooks with little sponges on them that you can dip in the sauce as needed. You can also make your own with an old dish sponge destined for the trash. Many of the pre-made sponge hooks have treble hooks which you probably want to avoid with children, so thread a sponge onto a circle hook yourself.

You can rig your bait several different ways, but most people choose to use a sinker of some sort to keep it near the bottom. My father used to rig these as a drop shot of sorts back before the technique became popular. He'd use a stringer hook (a hook that's connected to a leader with a loop at the end) and connect it to the middle of a section of line about 2' long. This set up is called a dropper loop rig and is quite common.

Dad would make an important modification that helped him fish this rig with three kids to attend to. Instead of tying this rig directly to the main line, he pre-rigged several of them a few days in advance. He would add a barrel swivel to the top of the dropper loop rig and would tie a snap swivel onto his main line, so all he would have to do was connect the two. You will, of course, want to use beefier snap swivels and barrel swivels if you're targeting giant fish. Being able to quickly swap out rigs was important, as these would often snag. Tying on a new snap swivel to the main line is much quicker than trying to tie an elaborate rig.

While Dad used to tie these with stringer hooks, a better option today is to use circle hooks so that the chances of gut-hooking and killing a fish is decreased. You could still tie the exact same rig but just use circle hooks instead. Just remember to reel in to set the hook rather than trying to set it with one jerking motion. This isn't a bad thing with younger kids, because they tend to just start reeling in, anyway.

Most of the time that you're using a sinker rig of some sort, you're fishing from shore or while anchored. It might increase your catch rate to move around a little bit throughout the day, but this can be tough on popular waters where everyone claims their favorite section of bank early, and nearly impossible if you have to convince your kids to come along too, especially if the panfish are biting where you're currently sitting. They might be wiser – one should "never leave fish to find fish," after all.

If you're in a boat, you might want to employ some sort of float rig instead, so that you can cover water easily while drifting and keep your bait presentable and unfouled by weeds. To tie a float rig you'll want a bobber of some sort (most prefer slip bobbers – ask your tackle shop to point you towards them) above your main rig. You'd usually only have one line extending from the bobber and the hook would be at the bottom of this line. You can also use these rigs to drift your bait down a river past a laydown or other cover that you think holds catfish.

You may still need some weight to keep your bait down, especially in a river current where the flow of water might push it towards the surface. They sell little sinkers for this that are malleable and clamp on your line. These are called split shot and almost look like big BBs with a slice cut from the middle. You just place the line in this slice and then pinch them down. Depending on the size of bait, flow of current, or other factors, you may need split shot. They're just as easy to remove, so it's easy to experiment with these.

If you want to target fish towards the middle of a river but find that your lure gets dragged towards you and shore, consider investing in a few planer boards. These are more often used while trolling to move lures out to the side and away from your boat wake, but they also work for bringing a lure out further from the bank in a river's current.

Regardless of if you're in a boat or fishing from shore, there is one piece of equipment that is absolutely vital if you're going to leave a rod waiting for a big one while you concentrate on helping your kids catch numbers of panfish: a good, solid, rod holder or some jury-rigged "seatbelt" of sorts. If you don't plan on having someone or something holding that rod when a big cat bites, you can plan on losing that combo to the deep.

Rod holders are the easiest if you have a place to screw them down, such as on a boat or your own dock. They are designed to keep your rod elevated so that anything pulling down on the lure, such as a fish, cannot pull the rod from the holder (just make sure the holder is locked if it's a model that swings – I've made that mistake before!). They don't cost very much and will pay for themselves the first time they save your combo from a large fish's tug.

Many boats these days have some sort of track system specifically designed for adding accessories like rod holders or down riggers, and even if they don't, screwing these in would be worthy holes for the boat, as you can use these holders for trolling too.

If you're fishing from a random shoreline, you obviously won't have a place to screw in a rod holder. You could get creative, and screw these into a few 2x4 boards that you carry along, but you're more likely to keep your rod in the air with some sort of forked stick. This is all well and good for keeping the rod tip high, but it won't do much to keep the rod on land if a big fish starts pulling. You're going to need to jury-rig some sort of "seatbelt" or safety device. It doesn't need to be complicated – a long piece of strong rope tied from the reel seat to a stout tree would work just fine. You just need something that will give you a chance to notice and react before your combo gets dragged in. You could also leave the bail open, but you'll need to rig a bell to warn you of fish.

I've had the best luck fishing for catfish and bullhead in the spring around Memorial Day, mostly because the water level tends to be high at that time and so these fish come closer to shore. With that said, catfish move about a lot during this time, so they aren't always where you want them to be. They are, however, renowned for their sense of smell, so if it's legal to chum and you are patient, you can usually call in a few. You'll have better luck if you can find some stable weather this time of year, but that can be tough, especially up north in the spring. Work schedules don't always permit taking your kids out fishing, but if you can sneak in some paid time off after two to four days of stable weather, your odds will improve.

This pair of channel catfish were a result of flooded waters and warm temperatures around Memorial Day of 2011. Every now and then, the parents need to catch one!

Like many other fish, catfish find deeper holes to hide in during the summer, though they'll move a bit shallower during the twilight. The nice part about summer is that the fish become more predictable. They aren't covering as much water as in spring and will typically set up in certain areas to ambush their prey. You'll find them holding near good cover that breaks up inbound current or flow. During summer, you're more likely to catch catfish during low light conditions such as dawn and twilight, though these can be tough times to have your kids out.

As the water cools during the fall, catfish tend to move towards deeper holes, especially in rivers. They'll stack up in certain ones and the fishing can be tremendous if you can figure out which spot they want. Unfortunately, many rivers out there aren't documented by sonar maps given that they can be inaccessible for large boats, so it can be tough to find these pools without help from some locals. A plus about fishing in the fall is you may have the area largely to yourself, so at least you can move around on shore more looking for fish as most of the community holes will be unclaimed even later in the day.

Catfish can be caught while ice fishing, but they won't be as shallow as you'd find them during the spring and summer. They're looking for warmer water and in the winter that means deeper water in many places – some 20' to 30' in natural lakes, and usually along ledges. The fishing will be slower in the winter, but remember, everything must eat eventually. Although rivers are popular places to fish for catfish, I would not recommend ice fishing on a river, even if others are doing so. Rivers have current and if something goes wrong, it goes very wrong. You can't count on simply bobbing in the newly created hole, and instead may be carried far away under the ice. I'm sure there will be plenty who say it's perfectly safe, but I am cautious with my kids and am unwilling to risk it.

Bullhead follow similar patterns to their larger cousins, but you'll tend to find them even shallower as they don't mind murky, mucky water. In many lakes they are far more common. They become quite easy to catch at night if you can stand the mosquitos. Just remember to read the section in Chapter 3 about unhooking bullhead safely as they can leave a nasty welt.

All in all, catfish and bullhead make for a great "bonus fish" while targeting panfish with your kids. They fight a bit harder and are a little more interesting to see, so they can be a nice kicker for the day, and they aren't that difficult to catch, assuming they're in the area.

Chain Pickerel

When your kids can cast a good 30' on their own with some regularity and control, they're ready to start fishing spinnerbaits for chain pickerel. These closely resemble smaller pike and put up a great fight on lighter tackle. They're voracious feeders and fairly easy to catch on fast-moving lures once the water temps start to climb to about 60°. Unlike pike, they don't all vanish to deeper haunts during the summer, which makes them good year-round targets.

Chain pickerel are great fish to target with slightly older kids who tire quickly of smaller panfish. While a three-year-old could catch bluegill and yellow perch until their arms fell off, such small offerings are unlikely to hold a preteen's attention for long. I'd still recommend starting after the little fish with the preteen just so they can have some success, but you want to move to try and "upgrade" quicker.

My son calls pickerel "boo boo fish" because I've taught him to be wary of their sharp teeth. You'll want to read "Holding Fish Safely" in Chapter 3 for information on how to hold these without being hurt, and you should never let a small kid attempt to grab them. I've found that pickerel have a nasty habit of thrashing worse than most fish after you take them into a net or lift them into a boat. Sometimes I think they fight harder after they're caught!

I mentioned in Chapter 3 that braided line can cause some nasty cuts, and most of them that I've suffered have come while dealing with pickerel. These fish thrash about so much that I'll try and grab the line to steady them a bit before I grab them by the back of the head or the gill plate. Without fail, the fish will start thrashing wildly while I'm holding the line, and if it's braid, that usually means I get a nasty cut. I keep telling myself that I'll stop doing this and I keep forgetting. I thought I'd mention it as sometimes kids don't want to hold a fish for a picture and will hold the line instead. I wouldn't recommend doing that with chain pickerel.

You'll find chain pickerel throughout the spring, summer, and fall in shallow grass flats. Whereas with pike you'd look for water 8-12' deep, pickerel are perfectly at home in the 2-6' range. I've also caught many pickerel over the years on laydowns and other wood cover, but I haven't found too many of them on rocky points like pike.

I tend to find pickerel closer to shore early in the year, but don't be afraid to fancast the entire flat. There are more than a few bays in Lake

Champlain around Crown Point and Ticonderoga where anglers will constantly beat the banks and reed edges looking for fish. Soon enough this pressure on the fish leads the bite to stop, but the anglers keep trying. While they're spinning their wheels, I've found great success casting towards open water, over the grass flats.

Pickerel will often patrol in the 4' to 6' range that you find a bit deeper and will hit flashy spinnerbaits with vigor. It might just be a result of all the pressure that the banks get, but I tend to catch most of my pickerel out a bit further in the bays. The water isn't appreciably deeper, but the fishing pressure is significantly relaxed.

I've had success trolling for pickerel along these same flats, though you'll probably want to find deeper water as the year progresses, just so you can avoid fouling in the weeds. I like dragging a ½ ounce spinnerbait or two behind my boat, either using planer boards or right behind me. When I don't use planner boards, I make a long cast, pull off another 10-15' feet of line, stick the rod butt in the rod holder and have my lunch while waiting for a bend.

You can successfully troll at speeds from 1.5 mph all the way up to 4 mph to draw strikes. Pickerel and their northern pike cousins seem to enjoy chasing their food. They are both quite capable of reaching speeds well in excess of 4 mph, so even though you think you're moving fast, your bait is still liable to be attacked. Vary your speed until you figure out how fast you need to go to keep your weed running true and weedless while staying in this range.

Trolling is a great way to fish while feeding your little one their lunch as once you get things set up and situated you can relax a bit and not have to work so hard at re-rigging. It can be a bit of a challenge to teach small children what a fish is compared to a weed – you're looking to see the rod bend over with authority and stay bent – not just bend a bit and spring back. Once they see a fish or two and what the strike looks like, they'll figure it out, but until that happens be prepared for them to run over and start reeling every few moments!

Trolling is also a great option for those kids who haven't quite got the hang of casting, or for days where they just aren't biting as well. You can cover water trolling much quicker than you can by casting. Many people will say to troll along break lines or depth changes when possible and I wouldn't argue with them, but the main flats that I patrol really don't change their depth much for a few hundred yards and I've found pickerel stacked throughout this range. I would argue that the primary concern is finding ambush routes and clear water between weeds where they can use their speed to their best advantage to strike.

The author as a child with a chain pickerel.

Pickerel are like pike and musky in that they'll follow lures all the way to the boat, often striking it within inches. This can be exhilarating but also presents a challenge in handing the rod off as there isn't much line for your kids to reel! Even so, a fish on for a few seconds is better than none so be aware of this behavior and keep your line in the water all the way to the boat. You can attempt a figure 8 (driving your rod tip into the water and making a figure 8 with it to try and entice a strike) but if you're fishing pickerel, you're probably in too shallow of water for this to be advisable or have much chance of success. I don't bother.

Chain pickerel will eat almost anything, but their very sharp teeth makes it difficult to land them when fishing slower lures because they often take these fully into their mouths and cut the line if you aren't using a leader. You'll find that you lose a lot of plastic worms and drop shots if pickerel are nearby.

They're also very frustrating if you're trying to fish a frog, because their hard, bony, tooth-lined mouths don't take such lures very well, though they'll come up and smash them. You can tell it was a pickerel that went after a frog both because the frog will be sliced up and leaking, and also because the pickerel tends to jump almost like a dolphin, cutting through the air horizontally and gracefully and then entering the water again. Bass tend to strike more vertically. It can be very frustrating trying to fish a frog pattern in pickerel-infested waters, but then again, this shouldn't be much of a problem for you when you have your kids with you as frogs aren't recommended lures for children in the first place.

If you want to avoid bite offs, your better option is to use fast-moving lures like spinnerbaits, swim jigs, and swimbaits to draw a reaction strike. Which lure you use is mostly going to depend on the weed cover.

Swimbaits usually but not always have exposed hooks that makes them difficult to fish near weeds – you really need to find the open lanes. Swimbaits are the most natural looking of the three options and come in more detailed color schemes, such as yellow perch (a favorite food of pickerel). Depending on the model, some swimbaits can be tough to burn in as they can flop around a bit and lose their action if retrieved too fast. Others are just fine at speed. I'd recommend those ones as speed often is the key. You might want to use a leader with these as there is nothing protecting the line and when fish eat these, they tend to slam them.

Spinnerbaits are the gold standard and do better in weedy water than the swimbaits. As stated earlier, this is because the bent wire frame in front of their hook does a decent job of deflecting some of the weeds before they can snag. Spinnerbaits come with a few different types of blades and many colors, but I prefer silver double willow blades matched to a white-skirted spinnerbait most days as I think it does a good job of looking like a fleeing baitfish. I will, on occasion, switch to a darker color like black or red if the skies are very overcast, or chartreuse if the water is very murky.

The bent wire frame of a spinnerbaits also does a pretty good job of defending the line from sharp teeth, so you can usually get away with fishing these without a leader. In all my years of fishing, I've only lost perhaps a half dozen spinnerbaits to pickerel and pike, usually because they bit it as soon as it hit the water and caught it at a weird angle.

I find swim jigs to be great for slipping through heavier weeds. They are a smaller bait than spinnerbaits and even though the latter's bent wire frame does a good job of deflecting some lighter weeds, it will certainly foul up in heavy ones. The swim jig doesn't have this problem and can often come through unscathed. It basically is a spinnerbait without the frame or the blades, so it's a more subtle presentation that can work better if there is heavy fishing pressure. You may want a wire leader with these however as they are very small (usually much smaller than swim baits) and are more likely to produce cutoffs if you're not careful.

All three of these lures (usually) have one thick hook which makes them safer for fishing with children. Although these hooks normally require a hefty hookset (which can be difficult for kids), fish tend to hook themselves on these lures as they hit them so aggressively while the lures are moving very fast (it still wouldn't hurt to set the hook for good measure, but your kids will catch plenty of them without this).

I've had several days out there on the water where chain pickerel were the only fish that bit. You can more or less count on them consistently and any 2' long fish will put just as large a smile on your toddler, so consider trying for a few after you fill your livewell with some panfish for the kids to play with while they're waiting for a bigger fish to strike.

Largemouth Bass

If you're an American or at least living here, then the largemouth bass is probably the reason you're reading this book as it's the most popular gamefish in the United States. Bass are also one of the main fish responsible for the prevalence of fishing books these days. If it weren't for ol' bucket mouth, fishing would not be nearly as scientific or thoughtful as it is today.

The largemouth bass has an extensive range throughout the United States and can be found a short drive away from most anglers. It can survive in small farm ponds, giant natural lakes, rivers, and man-made reservoirs.

It shares its habitat with many panfish and can often be caught while fishing for them. Your kids will tangle with one before you know it, and when they do, it's worth celebrating and taking a photo. Make a big deal out of even the smaller bass that your kids catch, as it's a legitimate gamefish.

*Largemouth bass are a great "bonus fish" for
kids as they are often found near the
panfish you're primarily targeting.*

Largemouth bass will hit a variety of lures that are good for
children. Spinnerbaits, swim baits, and swim jigs will catch them
almost as often as they'll catch chain pickerel, and in the same areas
and fashion.

Soft plastic worms and stick baits are big producers. I prefer to rig
them "wacky style" whenever I can get away with it without snagging
as bass seem to love the action of these falling through the water. I
find that I don't need to give these a lot of action if I cast them near
enough to a bass for them to notice, so this is a great technique for
kids. Just have them cast it out and let it fall. Most bites will come on
the fall. If not, have your kid give it a few twitches now to get it off
the bottom and heading towards the boat. Reel in the slack as you go.
While certainly not as simple as the "cast it out and reel it in" technique
that they'd use with a spinnerbait, it isn't rocket science and kids are
able to pick it up quickly enough (for that matter, they *could* also just
cast it out and reel it in – that will also often work).

If your child really wants to reel in the worm, the better option
would be to rig a Texas Rig, as this will allow it to slide through weeds

or other obstacles without fouling. The Texas Rig does have a drawback in that you bury the hook inside the worm, and a hookset can be necessary to release it and stick the fish, but if your kid is reeling it in fairly quickly, the fish will tend to hook themselves much like they do with a spinnerbait.

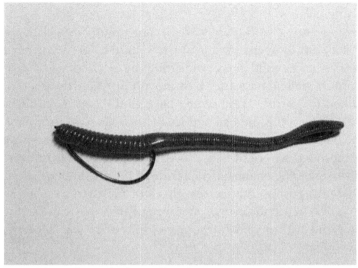

A Texas Rig is fairly weedless, but requires a good hook set to drive the hook through the worm and into the fish's jaw.

Another technique that I find catches a lot of largemouth bass are drop shot minnows, especially when the bite is slow. This is an easy enough presentation for children to use as all they need to do to work it is to cast it out, let it sink, and give it a few tiny taps – tap, tap, tap – before reeling in a foot or two and repeating the process.

There are hundreds of other ways to catch largemouth bass, some of which are a ton of fun for parents, but likely to frustrate smaller children (jigs and frogs come to mind). Even so, it wouldn't be the worst idea in the world to learn a bit more about the other lures out there in case you need to try to put your kid on a bass while they're having a break and some apple juice, so try to learn a few more of these techniques when you get a little time to fish by yourself. If your kids really take to fishing and want to make something of it on the tournament scene, they'll want to know about these other techniques, so the more you can learn about them yourself, the better.

Largemouth bass love live bait just like any other fish. Juvenile largemouth will strike the same cut up worms that you're using for panfish, but they prefer a juicier offering. If you notice that there are some bass in the area, I suggest rigging up a full worm as they'll have a hard time resisting. Make sure you let the worm's tail dangle off enticingly rather than balling it all up on the hook like you might do for smaller fish. Bass seem to prefer the action of a larger worm with a flowing tail.

Live minnows work very well for largemouth, especially when the bass stack up in deeper water in the summer. Some of my fondest memories as a child were of sitting by a deep pocket on Lake Champlain, pulling bass after bass in with the same dropper loop rig I described for catfish. Dad would have all three of us in his boat and all we'd do was flip the bail and let the bait keep on dropping until it hit the bottom. It wasn't long after that we'd feel a tug, and if we found a concentrated school of fish, this could repeat itself for hours.

That schooling characteristic is one of the great things about bass — they tend to group up at certain times of the year, so when you find one, you'll often find several. Because of this, they can be one of the easier game fish to find for your children once you know where to look.

In the spring, your search is going to start in one of two places: rocky points, or shallow bays. As the water starts to warm and approaches 55° - 60°, largemouth tend to group on rocky points that have flat spawning bays nearby. This is called the pre-spawn and it can be the best bite of the year but can be hard to time correctly as it can take place in a brief window, and often relies on a few days of calm weather. Not all fish spawn or stage for spawning at the same time, either, so be prepared to find your favorite rocky point vacant even if all the cards seem like they should align.

Once the waters warm a bit more (usually 60° to 65°) largemouth bass start to spawn. They prefer sandy bottoms in protected bays when available, and you'll often find them in areas that are flooded from spring rains and melting snow. An enormous amount of bass can inhabit the same area if the conditions are right, and you can really clean up by throwing plastic worms to likely ambush points or nests.

As discussed in the panfish chapter, it's easy to spot these nests. In clear water you might spot a circular, sandy clearing along the bottom. In murkier water you just need to look for the schools of panfish that are hovering in certain areas. They are right near a bass nest. If you can't spot the panfish because of the lighting conditions and water quality while they're still, you'll surely notice them after the largemouth parents take a run at them and cause them to leap from the water for their lives.

Fishing for bass on the beds is an ethical dilemma that can be a legal one depending on your state. As mentioned, most northern states (or at least the ones people would normally want to travel to for fishing adventures) protect this species during the spawn. Some allow no fishing for the largemouth during this vulnerable period, while others only allow a catch and release season.

If you're following my method of seeking panfish first and all other fish second, you're doing the bass a favor by removing some tormenting bluegills. Even if you do occasionally catch a bedding bass in the process, so long as you get them back in the water after a quick photo, I wouldn't lose any sleep.

The preparation for, and act of, spawning takes a lot out of bass, and the need to guard their nests against relentless attacks takes even more from them. Sometimes, this will lead to a decrease in activity immediately after the spawn and fishing can be tough. The good news is that the spawn isn't by calendar date and instead several other factors, so if you find that you're having trouble finding willing fish in one bay, simply move to another where you might have better luck.

In summer, largemouth bass enter relatively stable patterns where they can be caught with regularity, but again, only if you know where to look. Like in spring, many will frequently inhabit the same areas as panfish, so your kids should continue to catch them now and then as a byproduct or bonus fish. Substantial docks are a great place to find them, as are weed beds full of lily pads. Basically, anything that provides shade and cover has a good chance of holding bass.

Although plenty of bass can be found in the shady shallows during the summer, many others go deep as they chase various bait fish. When targeting such deeper bass, try a drop shot or using dropper loops as described above. If your lake has white perch, you can expect to pick up many of these as well, which might be a pain for the tournament fisherman but is an absolute blessing for a parent looking to delight their kids.

If you're fishing from a boat, use your fish finder to locate schools of large fish near underwater humps or ledges. This can be a fun activity in and of itself for your kids, as once you show them what a fish looks like on the finder, they will enjoy looking for them. Just be aware that kids are prone to mashing buttons and sending all your carefully preset conditions to shambles. Always remember, the more expensive the tool, the quicker a toddler will break it!

As summer cools down and fall approaches, the weeds will start to die off. Bass that held shallow will start following the surviving weeds which means they head to slightly deeper water. This signals that the water is about to turnover. Turnover is a complicated concept for this book, so suffice it to say that the warmer surface water cools enough to mix with the deeper water. This mixing throws things in a lurch for a week or two as it's a little bit like trying to move from one house to another. If you've ever done that, you know it throws you into disarray for a short while. Fish are no different. It can be tough to catch them at this time, but if you find this is your only week of vacation, don't despair. Remember, everything must eat.

If you can stick this period out or return a few weeks later, the fishing can be phenomenal. Bass will continue to follow the remaining weeds which will continue to concentrate them. They'll start feeding more aggressively to prepare for the long winter ahead and large catches are common. The water is cooler, and you'll need to bundle up the little ones, but fall can be a great time to take them out.

As ice forms on the lake, Largemouth bass can continue to be taken, though I'd venture to say they usually aren't the main target of many ice fishermen. Largemouth are a warm water fish, which means in the winter they'll be very deep as it's warmer down there than it is at the surface when the lake is frozen. You'll find they don't move much and won't be nearly as active as they would during the summer, but, again, everything must eat. Your best bet are live minnows fished right near the bottom. You want to make it as easy as possible for the bass to take them. Make sure you instruct your kids to set the hook as soon as they feel a bite because you can't count on the bass to swim very far with the meal and hook itself.

Later in the winter, right about when you're dreaming of spring, bass will start to congregate along drop-offs leading to spawning bays. If you can find these congregations, you can have a pretty good day with the kids. Just be sure the ice is still safe.

All in all, largemouth bass are a fairly common fish to catch and certainly among the best researched, meaning that there are plenty of resources out there beyond this book to assist you in learning more about the fish and catching more and more. They're a great fish to target as your child grows beyond the stage where you need to catch a fish, any fish, as fast and often as possible.

As your children mature and become more patient, you can use this fish to spark a love of reading in your kids and build their capacity for strategic thought. I used to really enjoy sitting with my dad and going through an old fishing book or magazine the night before our fishing trip and trying to figure out what we should do first. Fishing with your kids doesn't just build memories on the water. The entire vacation, from first light until bedtime can be special.

Smallmouth Bass

In his 1881 work, *Book of the Black Bass*, James Henshall famously wrote that smallmouth bass were, "inch for inch and pound for pound, the gamest fish that swims." It's hard to find someone who has tangled with the old bronze back and will disagree with him.

It's impossible to forget the first time you hook a smallmouth bass. These acrobatic fish are like miniature tarpon in that they fling themselves out of the water repeatedly, giving it their best go to shake the hook and free themselves. If they're not jumping, they're taking long, deep runs to try and snap your line. This fish has no quit and will give everything it has to the fight.

As you can imagine, this makes it an exciting fish to target with kids! Smallmouth aren't extremely large fish, so smaller tykes can handle them well, but they'll give them a good fight and a great memory.

They're also ideal for children in that they can be caught with many of the rigs and approaches that I consider "child friendly." They'll hit all the same stuff a largemouth will, but they're especially prone to biting a minnow on a drop shot.

The smallmouth's range is primarily the Midwest to Northeast United States although there have been stockings in several western impoundments and reservoirs. They are prevalent in the Great Lakes and many fishing tournaments revolve around who can catch them there.

I often find smallmouth in deeper water than largemouth. If you're following the maxim of seeking panfish first, this can still work, especially if your lake has white perch as they are a rather large species of panfish that tends to inhabit the same areas smallmouth.

The exception to this deeper water tends to be in the spring when smallmouth come in to shore to spawn. Unlike largemouth bass, smallmouth don't usually spawn so much in shallow, weedy bays as they would prefer areas with a lot of rocks, gravel, and other rubble. This is, of course, if such cover is available. If not, weedy bays will do just fine.

You can usually spot their prime spawning territory from a boat or shore, because shorelines tend to reflect what will be under the water nearby. If you see many rocks on the shore, there are probably rocks in the nearby water. Look for such areas that are protected from most wave action as these fish prefer to spawn in areas that aren't going to rock back and forth every time a storm comes along.

While searching for likely congregations, bear in mind that you don't always have to find the shallowest water lined with rocks. While it's true that smallmouth will often nest in 2-5 feet of water, they've also been observed at 20 feet or so. It all seems to depend on the water clarity and ability of the sun to reach them.

A good-sized smallmouth will give kids a great-sized fight.

While you'll hear many anglers excitedly talk about "the bass being on the beds," it's actually the pre-spawn period that has the best fishing of the year, as the fish will be gearing up for what is to come and eager to eat.

In the north, this will happen sometime between late April and June as the surface water temperature approaches 45° – 55°. You'll find groups of fish concentrated and the fishing can be incredible. Your best luck will come after a period of some stable weather.

The spawn itself (around 55° to 65°) is a period of a few days where the fish are busy making babies and unlikely to strike a lure unless it really aggravates them. For the future sake of the species, let them do their thing and have their fun and find another fish to catch – the lake is full of them.

The post-spawn period is, as with largemouth bass, a difficult time to catch fish as they tend to be exhausted from the ritual. Males will guard their nests (meaning, coincidentally, that there are panfish to guard them from, which is a good thing if you're fishing with kids, as the panfish remain easy targets), but most females disappear to deeper water and become difficult to catch. No matter, as you're chasing quantity vs. quality when with kids.

As the waters warm and spring turns to summer, fishing can either be excellent or challenging. On the one hand, this is the time of year when the most prey is available, the most eating is done, and the most growth occurs for fish. On the other, there is *so* much prey available that feeding windows are often condensed. Summer is the reason anglers get up before dawn. The bite is significantly better in the morning (and again in the evening) than it is during the day.

Another challenge for fishing during the summer is that smallmouth bass become much less concentrated, meaning you'll need to cover much more water to find them. This is simply because there are so many good spots for them to hang out. There's no hard and fast rule that only one fish can be in a certain area, however, so if you find habitat that can support several them, you'll still be able to pull several out of an area. Bridge pilings, larger rock formations and sunken islands and deep weed beds are all good places to look.

The same turnover period that affects largemouth bass behavior will also turn off smallmouth fishing, and perhaps more so as the smallmouth tends to be deeper and thus more likely to be in water that is severely affected by the event. If you find yourself in this situation, it's recommended that you go to the shallows as those waters are not going to be as changed and turbulent.

The best day of smallmouth fishing that I've ever had was in the fall, and several guides that I know make these their prime target that time of year. The fish are again concentrated and catchable as they are bulking up for the winter.

I can't just mention my best day of smallmouth fishing without going into it a bit. It was mid-September 2011 on Lake Champlain. It was a very unusual year as the lake had flooded in the spring to record levels (103.57 feet at Whitehall, NY compared to the average 95.5 feet). The water started high, so it stayed high all year, but this was compounded by Hurricane Irene which arrived that August. While it didn't directly hit upstate New York and Vermont, there was enough residual rain and runoff that the lake maintained a very high level well into the fall.

This created a situation where the water near the creeks in Ticonderoga and Crown Point were considerably higher than they usually are. For example, the mouth of Putnam Creek is usually a boating hazard this time of year given there are sand bars to its north and south. The higher water levels meant that this entire area remained accessible and the smallmouth arrived in numbers. A group of three or four boats including my own just formed a big circle and cast into this area, at times pulling in a smallmouth each cast. It was a good lesson in how concentrated this fish can be in the right situation.

Back to the seasonal patterns, a smallmouth is no different than any other creature in that it must eat, and it will continue to do so in winter as the lakes freeze. Even so, just like largemouth bass, smallmouth bass are not exactly the prime target for most ice anglers. If you insist on trying, look for them on deeper sunken islands and rocky breaks and offer them smaller morsels and jig heads as they are finicky.

As with largemouth, smallmouth bass (or at least the small ones) can be easy fish to catch and inhabit areas that also hold panfish, which makes them a nice bonus catch when fishing with your children. Their acrobatic displays and hard-fighting qualities are sure to make them a favorite with your kids, and lead to several joyous giggles and hollers.

Because smallmouth bass are another accepted catch in bass tournaments, plenty has been written about them to help anglers succeed. This means that they too are a good way to spark your children's love for reading. It's a nice perk and a good thing to help you sell the necessity of your latest fishing trip and expenditures to your significant other.

Northern Pike

These massive, hard-fighting fish are what I'd consider the "end boss" for teaching your kids how to fish. They are the crème de la crème of sportfish in northern waters and the largest predator your child is likely to tangle with. True, there is a larger species called the Muskellunge, but these are known as the "fish of 1,000 casts," which makes them the virtual antithesis of a fish you should target with young children! Northern pike will have to do for your finale!

Northern pike have a range that extends across the northern hemisphere of the globe with great fishing in Russia, Europe, and North America. They grow considerably larger overseas as well - just something to keep in mind if you're ever across the pond and want to take the kids out for a little nature walk along some shore.

These fish put up a tremendous fight and your child will have all they can deal with. You might need to help them hold the rod on occasion lest it be ripped from their hands. If they're small, it's going to be very difficult for them to hold their rod tip up high and they're going to need a lot of encouragement. It's very important that they don't give these fish any slack because that may cause the lure to move just enough for the fish to spit it out, or its teeth to cut the line.

You'll find pike in the same type of habitat as you found pickerel, but further out where the water is deeper. Weeds in water depths of 8' to 12' range are ideal, especially if there is a mixture including some cabbage. Pike also enjoy having deeper, cooler water nearby to escape to during the heat of the day.

I've found that the best place for pike is near the mouth of a creek that spills out into a grass flat with deeper water nearby. There are several creeks in southern Lake Champlain, and most will hold pike nearby throughout much of the year. They aren't always going to be right in the creek mouth, but you'll often find them nearby. Creek mouths have current, which predators enjoy, and they also tend to have cooler (and often clearer) water flowing from them. This change in water clarity and temperature can really stack up fish.

Northern pike are the "end boss" for fishing with kids on many northern lakes.

Much of the same techniques that work for pickerel will work for the larger members of the *Esox* family as well. Spinnerbaits are an especially productive lure when burned in fast. A traditional lure for catching these fish would be large spoons and even larger jerkbaits (sometimes the size of your forearm), but both would be difficult and dangerous for a young child to use as they have sharp treble hooks. On the other hand, the treble hooks on the more gargantuan jerkbaits are about as thick as your standard spinnerbait's hook, anyway, so they're not as dangerous. Regardless, such lures are completely impractical for a smaller child and I'd bet your kid gets tired of tossing these massive lures after one or two retrieves.

Trolling techniques utilized for pickerel will also work for pike. Again, you want to target a bit deeper water. In fact, you might go so far as to target very much deeper water and use deep-diving plugs or considerably heavier spinnerbaits in search of northerns during the summer months. Just stay near drop-offs next to a weed line for some good action.

If your kids are old enough to cast, that can be the best fun of all because to feel the strike from one of these monsters is to know what it's like to live. In clear water, you often get to see the slashing attack as well. There's nothing quite like a massive silver flash intercepting your spinnerbait and it's mesmerizing how they can rocket from the depths and stop elegantly on command to engulf your offering. Twitching the rod a bit as you retrieve a spinnerbait quickly is key to calling up these fish as they'll often hit it on the pause or twitch. If you're trolling, vary your speed from time to time.

These fish can be taken on live and dead bait as well though they prefer larger offerings and sometimes take a bit of skill to hook. They'll often hit the bait sideways and you'll need to give them a moment to position it in their mouth appropriately so you can hook them. Basically, you just give them a few seconds after they strike before you set the hook.

Spring is one of the best times to catch these fish because the cooler water brings them shallower, and the needs of nature makes them hungry. Very large pike can be taken shallow early in the year but as stated earlier you're going to need to move back towards the deeper water as things get warmer.

Summer can be a tough time to find these fish, or at least the true trophy ones, but you'll still find plenty of smaller ones in the same 8' to 12' weed flats and ridges, and even a smaller pike is still going to get your kids screaming with excitement.

My personal best pike have come in the fall. The waters cool again, and the impending winter convinces the pike that it's time to start gorging again to fatten up for the lean months ahead. Spinnerbaits work very well this time of year, especially if you can get a few days of calm and stable weather.

Pike are taken in large numbers by ice fishermen. They are a cold-water fish and remain active throughout the winter months. Again, you'll want to start with weed beds in large bays. Dead bait works very well this time of year, as you might expect.

As with pickerel, you're going to want to be cautious about letting your children hold these fish for a picture. The good news with pike at least is that they don't thrash nearly as much as pickerel do once they're in the boat, so you're less likely to tear your hands up on the fishing line, but they have just as sharp and even larger teeth to contend with all the same. These certainly aren't fish for toddlers to hold and you'll want to have mom or dad take care of that. If your little one brought one of these giants in, I'm sure you'll have no problem being included in that picture, smile beaming.

Bowfin

It's hard to find a fish people write less about than bowfin. This is a shame, because a bowfin is one of the hardest fighting, most fun fish you can catch, and a great one to target with your kids.

They range along much of the eastern United States from Florida through upstate New York and west to the Mississippi watershed wherever warm, shallow water can be found.

They are prehistoric monsters that date back from the time of the dinosaurs (seriously—they've been around for over 100 million years). They look ancient with a head that almost looks like a coelacanth, and if you see one lunge at a hooked fish near your boat, it'll give you quite a scare.

They're capable of breathing atmospheric air which means they can survive a long time out of the water. In my experience, this also means that they refuse to tire or give up fighting once you have them in the boat like some other fish. They have very sharp teeth and firmly belong in the "boo boo fish" category – don't let your child hold them.

The bowfin is much more popular in the south than the north but there are plenty of them up here as well. They tend to be a shallow water fish and will inhabit waters warmer and less oxygenated than most other fish can stand. Every now and then you'll see them cruising high in the water column, occasionally poking their nose out of the water to take a gulp of fresh air.

Much like gar, these fish cast huge shadows slowly moving through the water that are going to preoccupy your attention and cause you to cast to them. Unfortunately, much like gar, it can be very tough to entice them to bite! That doesn't mean you shouldn't try, as when they do bite, they bite ferociously and give a great fight.

You'll find that when a bowfin smashes a lure, that is the end of the lure. Spinnerbaits emerge from their maw a tangled mess of broken steel. Crankbaits and topwater lures are often crushed, with their hooks spread apart beyond hope. Great problems to have!

If you're fishing for bass or pickerel with your kids, you'll likely encounter a bowfin now and then as they do patrol the same shallow weed flats where you'll find the more popular gamefish. They'll hit "bass lures" from time to time and when they do, you'll wonder if you've hooked a monster pike. If you get one to strike a topwater, you'll think you've hooked a whale.

For me at least, bowfin tend to be accidental catches when fishing with artificial lures. When I'm targeting them deliberately, I'm using some form of live or dead bait. You can use the same rigs you'd fish for catfish and most of the same bait. Just throw it out there and let it soak. Unlike cats, bowfin will bite very well throughout the day, especially early in the spring. Our house has a dock that's in the middle of a shallow flat (2' – 5' of water most times of the year) and catching bowfin from it this way has been a long-held tradition.

A variety of fish, including a large bowfin (right),
caught from our dock when we were little.

I've had bowfin hit everything from live shiners to cut up hot dogs and found them both patrolling near our dock and taking refuge beneath it. If you have lakeside access near some shallower water, sometimes it can be fun to soak a few lines and see if you can put your kids on some larger fish. Just have them play a game or other sport while they're waiting for a bite.

Although your best bet is, in my opinion, always going to be some sort of bait, plenty of people take plenty of bowfin on lures. Some specialists use fly rods and larger flies to take them on topwater, which produces an acrobatic fight. Others swear by big purple worms, Texas rigged. Most of the bowfin I have caught on artificial have hit spinnerbaits and top water popper lures.

As bowfin prepare to spawn in the spring, their underside and fins turn a dazzling display of bright neon green or blue, making them even more interesting for kids. This is also one of the best times to fish for them, as they'll attack anything that gets close to their nests.

One thing you want to be aware of when fishing for bowfin is that they are not an invasive species – they are, however, commonly misidentified with northern snakehead which are an invader to be rooted out. The two don't look anything alike if you ask me. Snakehead are much darker fish and snakehead have a very long anal fin (the fin on their underside) that runs from about their midsection to their tail. Bowfin have a short anal fin, like a pickerel or pike. If you have any questions, please see your local fisheries manager before slaughtering a fish due to mistaken identity.

Walleye

If you're in the Midwest, you're probably itching to take your kids fishing for some walleye. They are the gamefish supreme out that way, and are popular enough that they, like bass, have spawned their own class of boats (let's be honest – a "multi-species boat" is really a boat designed to target walleye).

These popular gamefish are fun to catch and delicious to eat, and their large range (most of the interior of the United States and Canada) means that they are accessible to many anglers.

Walleye are an interesting fish in that their eyes are very sensitive to light, so they aren't always the best fish to target on the nice, sunny days you're hoping for on most vacations. Instead, you'll want to let your kids have a nice vacation treat and stay up late to go searching for some bites.

Most other factors that decrease light penetration into the water can favorably impact the bite. Choppy seas have a good way of doing this, if you and your kids can stand fishing in them. Silty water stirred up by the waves can bring these fish shallow to feed. You don't want it to turbid as there can be too much of a good thing, but it is interesting considering that many other species appear to prefer clearer water. The walleye, with their sensitive eyes seem quite at home within the murkiness. In fact, they have great night vision compared to other fish, which is something to consider if you ever want to take your (older) kids out in the moonlight for a true adventure.

Walleye will strike a variety of lures and bait, but you'll do best if you try to match the color patterns to what they're used to eating. In many northern realms, this means yellow perch. These panfish tend to inhabit the same general areas as walleye, though they're often schooled a short distance away and don't intermingle.

Other live bait that is popular for walleye include worms and leeches. Depending on your area, leeches can be hard to come by, but if your bait shop carries them, you can be in for a great day. Just make sure that the leeches look healthy and are active. These do work better in warmer water because when it's very cold, they tend to curl up and refuse to move.

Nightcrawlers also work but bear in mind that walleye are going to want a larger meal than panfish. As discussed, walleye and yellow perch tend to live near, but not on top of, each other. Thus, if you find your worm being hacked to shreds by little fish, try casting in a slightly different spot around the same structure.

If you prefer artificial lures, walleye can be caught on an excellent rig for young anglers – simple round head jigs, either topped with a grub of some sort, or bucktail. These lures are great for kids because they will catch panfish in addition to walleye, have a single hook less likely to grab them, and are pretty easy to use – cast them out, let them sink, and work them back in a series of hops.

Walleye will also go for a series of plugs, trolled or retrieved, but as these tend to have treble hooks, they're not recommended around younger, curious children.

These fish have predictable seasonal patterns. The same light-sensitivity tends to drive walleye a little deeper than several of the other fish mentioned in this book, though they will move up shallow in spring to spawn. They start moving in earlier than may other fish, though this depends on the latitude. Look for water temps around 40° – 44° for walleye to spawn in the north, and a bit higher in the south.

Interestingly, walleye do not spawn in the same shallow, protected areas as many fish, but instead prefer rocky shoals that are exposed to wind. They'll also stack up in such areas near small streams, apparently unconsidered or perhaps even drawn to the flowing water.

As with many fish, the spawning effort will exhaust walleye and make them difficult to catch, but this period only lasts a short time. Once they recover, they tend to hang around the same general area that they spawned for a short period, which can make the fishing fantastic with kids as the fish are shallower, easier to find, and eager to bite. Walleye appear to be consistent in that areas that held pre- and post-spawn fish one year tend to produce the next. This contrasts with bass who could be staging at any number of rocky points from one year to the next.

While walleye will remain in the shallows throughout much of the spring, they tend to move deeper in the summer as the sun rises higher and stays brighter day by day. Their exact depth will be determined to an extent by geography, as they tend to be deeper the further south in their range you go. This stands to reason given that the overall lake will be warmer in the south, so the cooler water will be deeper. Look for mid-lake humps, weed line edges, and rocky reefs near their preferred depths. The very end of an extended point can be a prime location.

Some walleye will return to the shallows during the fall as the surface water cools, and as there is less food to find anywhere else. You really do need to follow the bait and keep in mind that earlier and later in the year, most food sources are going to be shallow, whereas during the summer they can be anywhere.

Being great eating, the walleye is popular with ice anglers. Here too, you'll want to keep in mind the maxim of "find the bait, find the fish." Food is scarce in the winter and energy must be conserved. Most fish don't roam any further under the ice than necessary to find a meal. You'll find walleye in the same shallow weeds as their prey. If you can find such an area along a point with access to deeper water, you might be on a walleye gold mine.

While the walleye's light-sensitive nature can make them a little difficult to catch during prime kid hours, if you do find yourself with a choppy day or a night owl for a kid, they can make for a fun day and a great meal afterward.

*Walleye make for a fun adversary
and a delicious meal*

Others

To a child, a fish is a fish is a fish. They don't care what they catch, and for younger children at least, everything is a giant.

There's such a multitude of fish out there that it would be well beyond the scope of this volume to explore them all so I will instead leave you with some basic advice: when you hear about how some waterway has some crazy cool fish that you want to try and catch, think long and hard about just how easy it is to catch it, and if you're going to be able to catch panfish consistently while you search for your white whale.

Most of the fish described in this chapter can – at one point in the year or another – be targeted while fishing for panfish. That is what makes each of these "good" fish to seek with your kids. I haven't included popular fish like rainbow trout, lake trout, or salmon in this volume because to fish for such species would usually violate the rule of quantity. Unless you know your child is exceptionally patient, or they have been fishing long enough to endure a slower day, I advise you to stick to this rule.

You want unique species to be a nice bonus or "kicker" for your kids' day, not some white whale you pursue to your kid's exhaustion. The panfish keep them engaged and interested and agreeable and the occasional bass, walleye, pickerel, pike, musky, or bowfin is what cements that day in their memories. They rush home to mom or dad or their grandparents and talk about how they caught tons of fish, and even a big one! No, a HUGE one! That's a big deal – keeping them going for a long time without the constant panfish action is tough and likely counterproductive.

Bear that in mind while you're staying up late at night learning how to vertical jig for lake trout or use jerkbaits or stockings to go after longnose gar. Just because you can do something, does it mean you should if you have your kid with you? To find your answer, think about if they can frequently catch smaller fish while you're messing around for the big ones, and if the answer is "no," then pass on that adventure for the time being.

Longnose gar are impressive fish but a poor choice for targeting with small kids. Save the "exotics" for when they are older.

7 – PREPARING FOR THE DAY

The old maxim, "fail to plan, plan to fail" is just as true with fishing as any other pursuit in life, and it's only exacerbated when you start involving children in the sport. As you've learned from this book, there's a lot that goes into trying to help your children find success out on the water in terms of adjusting your attitude, setting expectations, purchasing and rigging a number of rods and reels with appropriate tackle, and having some idea about the seasonal patterns and behaviors of your quarry. Believe it or not, even after doing all these steps, your prework isn't complete.

Scouting

Lake Champlain has some of the best fishing on the planet, but it's far enough away that I can't get to it near as much as I'd like throughout the year. This means that every time I go there, I need to reinvent the wheel so to speak, and find fish over again. I can't easily track their movements like I can closer to home, because it's often weeks or months between trips, so I have very little idea where they are when I arrive. This is all part of the fun when fishing by myself or with my father, as one of the best parts of fishing is figuring stuff out. Unfortunately, that is a hard sell for my little ones, who expect constant action as soon as their line hits the water!

To accommodate them, I do the best I can to scout before we ever get there. The internet is a great source of knowledge that just gets bigger and better by the day. No matter where you're fishing, there's probably someone who has taken the time to post some fishing reports and tips recently. These can give you some great ideas for areas to fish, lures to use or different tactics to try.

If you can't find a recent report, don't be afraid to use ones from around the same time years ago. As discussed in Chapter 6, fish have predictable seasonal patterns. They will tend to go to the same general areas and have the same general behaviors from year to year. While you can't always count on this (more than a few fishing tournaments have been lost chasing yesterday's glory) it gives you a pretty good idea of where to start.

If possible, the best way to scout is to go out fishing by yourself before you bring your kids along. This is a great excuse to tell your significant other that you "have" to go fishing ahead of time "so the kids can be successful." Someone has to do it!

Your goal is not to catch every fish or even any fish – you just want to find them. Make sure that you bring a pair of polarized glasses to help you spot shadows and other activity. If the lake is clear enough, you might see the fish themselves, but if you can't, look for signs that they are there. Small fish jumping or making swirls in the water is a good sign as is the presence of fish-eating birds like herons – they aren't there to sight-see!

If you intend to fish from a bank, you'll want to walk around and look for good areas where you can fish successfully, safely and comfortably with your children. The places with the best access aren't always the best fishing spots, but you'll want to find at least enough of a clearing where young feet can move around without tripping and getting hurt.

You'll also want to make note of the weeds in the water. It won't do you much good to set up shop right in front of a matted mess of milfoil. You need to find areas with clear water where you can soak a worm without immediately fouling it. This will get more challenging as the year gets warmer and the weeds become more abundant.

Depth is also important. It will be tough to find many fish if the water is too shallow for too long. You'd be better off finding an area that is 3-4' deep for at least as far as your little one's casting range and then drops off.

To sum up the ideal bank location: it's a clear enough space for young kids to play and cast without catching trees constantly, the water has some depth to it, and there are weeds but also clearings to cast to.

An ideal location – deep enough to hold fish with ample weeds nearby, but a clearing where worms can sink, and children can cast.

A poor location – the shore has room to cast, but the weeds are matted to the surface. Even if there are fish, they'll be hard to catch.

Much the same applies when fishing from a boat though you'll probably want to know where the prevailing winds tend to come from on your lake and then check out a few bays where you can get out from them regardless of their direction. For example, the two most common wind directions on Lake Champlain are from the north and south, so it's important to know what bays protected from each look like in terms of weed growth and access. Having a few spots lined up will allow you to continue catching fish no matter what mother nature throws at you.

Regardless of if you're on a boat or beating the bank, you'll want to carry along a fishing rod equipped with a good search bait for panfish. My favorite method for this is a drop shot rigged with a small scented artificial minnow. I have confidence in this because it's what I go to for catching fish when nothing else works. It tends to draw in taps from panfish quickly enough if they're there. I catch enough fish with this throughout the year that I'm confident that if it isn't producing any taps, the fish just aren't there. This makes it easy to cover water quickly and figure out where to set up with nightcrawlers the next day when I bring the little ones along.

When I locate some fish with this method, I make a mental note of it and move on. I don't want to spoil the area for my kids by catching too many fish – I just want to know where they are so I can start off right the next day.

Chumming

Where legal, chumming can be a very effective tactic for bringing in panfish (and more)! Chumming is the process of throwing food out in the water to draw in fish over a period. It is not lawful everywhere, so you'll want to check your local regulations. If allowed, rabbit food works very well, as does oatmeal and corn.

Sustained chumming over a series of days can turn an otherwise average stretch of shoreline into one of the hottest sections of the lake. Panfish, bullhead, catfish, and bowfin are species that seem to be especially receptive to this tactic.

If you own a house on a lake where this is legal and can do this consistently, it's also a great way to increase the average size of the fish near your dock. I still fondly remember catching absolute monster bluegills in front of my uncle's house as a kid.

Setting Expectations for Your Kids

One of the more important steps of any fishing trip with kids is setting expectations for yourself and your children. It's a balancing act because you want to pump them up and get them excited for what's to come without setting the bar too high to reach. Where you intend to go and how the scouting went will play a big part in how much you cheerlead and what you promise.

You should never promise that you're going to catch a fish unless you are completely certain this is possible. Likewise, you should not promise a certain size, or species. Instead, you should just focus on all the cool stuff that you know is going to happen. Say things like, "I'm so excited to spend some time with you!" or "I'll bet we see a bunch of cool birds and frogs!" and "Maybe we'll even catch some fish!" At the end of the day, your kids adore you and just want to hang out with you. Little ones especially are very content to be given something to carry, "a job" to complete, and a role in the process to make them feel like a big kid. Catching fish is icing on the cake.

You could also say things like, "Hey, let's try fishing for a little while and then we'll get some ice cream!" Make sure there's a guaranteed treat in it for them before the day is done, so they're always looking forward to something in addition to the fishing in case it doesn't take off.

Taking this approach will remove a lot of pressure from the situation which in turn will mean you're less stressed, more focused, and more likely to catch something. I don't care what you're doing in life – taking a test, drafting a technical letter, or working a lure – if you're stressed out you aren't going to perform as well as if you're cool and confident.

Setting Expectations for Yourself

You also need to mentally prepare for a fishing trip with your kids. Regardless of if the fish are biting or not, you're in for quite the ordeal. Your day is likely to start with a little cloud of doubt following you around until the first fish is caught. You're going to need to stay positive and smiling and encouraging for your kids and keep them occupied for the first few minutes, even when they seem like hours.

You need to keep in mind that you're looking for quantity and not quality. I've been hammering that home throughout this book and there's a good reason for it. You need to remember that kids – scratch that, newcomers in general – don't care what size of fish they catch. If they've never caught a fish before, any fish seems like a monster. The tug on the line is all they crave – they don't have wild expectations for some giant catch.

I forgot this once a few years ago when I was taking my cousins out fishing. They weren't all that young at the time – maybe 12 and 15 or so, but they hadn't fished much. I made the mistake of assuming that because they were older, they weren't going to want panfish. This lead us around the lake a bit searching for larger quarry and generally boring them until we gave up on that and decided to just start catching fish – any fish.

Targeting the smaller fish paid off because it gave my cousins something to reel in. Their confidence started to take off. By going where the fish were located, we also started keying in on where some larger fish might also be. Soon enough, they were sticking pickerel with spinnerbaits and having a ball. It was slow going because I tried to jump right to that result instead of working our way into it. It's a good thing I changed it up or they would have lost interest.

When you take kids fishing, you're going to be constantly tasked with keeping a few lines operational and in the water, probably casting them repeatedly as your child reels it in immediately, not quite yet grasping the concept that they need to wait for a bite. Somewhere in the middle of this, you'll become engrossed by some task and not notice that your kid has picked up a rod. They'll do their best to mimic you and try to cast it. Their experiment will have a great chance of winding up in a tree, or as a snarled mess of a tangle. There's also the outside chance that you wind up with a new hook earing.

Even if things go exceptionally well and the fish are biting left and right, you're going to need to be at your absolute best. There are few things as hectic as fishing with a toddler when they're pulling them in one after the other. One moment you'll be casting a rod and as soon as you hand it off to your kid so you can pick up the second rod, a fish will be on. You'll cast the second rod out quickly just so you can get it out of your hands to start unhooking the first fish. Your kid will drop the first rod (almost hooking you in the process as it jerks the fish you're trying to release) and will go grab the second one – fish on again! This could keep going on for several minutes, with the only respite coming from the need to thread on a new worm. This will be hectic and push your patience, agility, and multitasking skills to the max, but it's very much what any parent would call "A good problem to have."

More likely, however, things will go wrong. You'll forget the worms at home and will need to repeatedly explain that to your son. Your daughter will kick a rod over in the lake while she's peering into the livewell. There will be temper tantrums and meltdowns just like any other day, but you'll already be completely stressed out and it will be vital that you react appropriately.

So, in short, set your own expectations – you will not relax during this trip, you will not catch a fish of your own during this trip, and you will probably be physically injured (at least a little) during this trip. If you can make it through without losing your footing on some moss and winding up in the drink, you're ahead of the game.

Distractions and Other Attractions

My four-year-old would stay outside fishing all day long if I let him. The biggest meltdown of the day is when I tell him it's time to come in for supper. He spends a good portion of the time with a rod in his hand, but I have found it's a good idea to keep some "distractions and other attractions" around to help the day go smoothly. Half the time these have very little to do with keeping him happy and very much to do with giving me a chance to get some tackle untangled or to get a good trolling pass set up.

My son absolutely loves putting panfish in the livewell on our boat and then opening it up and just lying there, looking at them from time to time and babbling to them or naming them. He has a little minnow net that he uses to take the fish out so he can throw them back in the lake, and this seems to be just as much fun for him as actually catching them. I had to buy him the net because before we had that he would just stick his hand in after them, jacket and all, and get completely soaked. Even now, if he's wearing sandals there's a good chance that he's going to try to stand in the livewell with the fish when I'm not looking.

I try to keep a lot of little snacks that take a bit of effort for him to finish nearby, such as an orange that needs peeling, or some crackers to dip in hummus. The snacks help him stay nourished and avoid crankiness, but the bigger plus is that they take him a few minutes to go through. This is my quiet time on the boat where I can either address tackle issues or even fish on my own for a bit, while I try to hook him a larger fish to reel in.

Electronics can also be helpful to have on the boat for emergencies. Yes, much of the point of taking them fishing is to get them away from the smart phone, but sometimes things go wrong to such an extent that the safest thing for them is to get drawn back in by a screen for a couple of minutes while you address the issue. It's very easy to break them away once the situation is at hand. I know I'm "not supposed" to recommend this, but you wouldn't want to leave the phone behind just to say you did, and you shouldn't feel bad if you have to use it for a few minutes here or there to gain control over a particularly bad situation like fishing line in the trolling motor, or removing a hook from your hand. Just make sure you aren't using it as a distraction so that you can fish for you.

When fishing from shore, it sometimes pays off to bring a bucket along even if you plan to release your fish as it can play the same role as the livewell above. Kids enjoy being able to run over and look at their fish whenever they need a break from fishing. Just make sure that you change the water frequently and keep the bucket in the shade, so you don't needlessly stress the fish. It should go without saying when placing fish in a bucket or livewell that they must be in season and of legal length. Possession is possession, even if the intent is to eventually release the fish.

If you can find a pond that has a nearby playground or interesting geography like some large rocks to play on, that would be ideal. Not every four-year-old is going to want to stay out all day and having the playground to fall back on is great for when the fish aren't biting. If there is no playground, a field and a ball can go a long way to salvaging a slow day.

When the fish are biting, don't be afraid to ask your kid if they'd like to try netting a few. Young children seem to find this just as enjoyable as catching the fish, and it'll give you an opportunity to reel a few in and keep your sanity. The trip is about putting a smile on their face, and it's important that you drop your preconceived notions about how that must be achieved.

Another great option is to bring along a small tackle box for your kid and fill it with some lures. Just make sure they're relatively safe. Occasionally my son will take a break from fishing and just play with some plastic worms, having one "talk" to the other. The conversations are fascinating.

Finally, if all else fails and you find yourself away from any other distractions, go nuclear: bring bubbles. Just don't do it on the boat unless you want to slip and fall into the lake.

Packing for the Day

In addition to whatever distractions you plan to bring, make sure that you use common sense and keep an eye on the weather to decide what you should bring along to keep your kids calm and comfortable.

Hats are a big deal as are sunscreen. The last thing you want to do is bring your kid home fried. They'll be miserable, your wife or husband will be angry, and you'll feel awful. Some kids hate putting on sunscreen, but you need to make it happen. Luckily, several children's stores stock sunhats and clothing that are rated to SPF 50 or higher, so the amount of skin you need to treat can be reduced. Even so, keep an eye on where they're sitting, what they're doing, and how this is causing the sun to hit them. If they're playing in the livewell, you might find you need to apply some lotion to their lower back even if they're wearing a shirt. Notice this early or you will be in for it.

Rain gear can be important for actual rain or even spray from the waves. Just remember that it does absolutely no good if you don't zip it up (something I learned the hard way one horribly cold autumn morning on Lake Champlain).

A cooler filled with goodies is key, and you can never have too much water. A rag or towel makes everything that much easier and cleaner. Some children will prefer to hold fish with these as it does make them less slippery and prone to stick them with their spines. Forgetting this stuff at the house tends to mean turning back early.

Oh, and for the love of all things good and sacred – don't forget to pack the worms!

Where & When to Start

Ok, so you've done your due diligence with scouting or chumming (where lawful), set modest expectations, planned for some distractions and packed a bag. It's finally time to go fishing! Now there's just one small problem: where oh where should you start? Fishing trips with children are not the time or place to try new things or test a theory. I would very much recommend trying to "get the skunk out of the boat" as soon as possible when fishing with kids, so your first stop should be the most likely place that a fish – any fish – will be. Learn from my near failure with my nephews discussed above and don't repeat my mistake – you're not looking for size – you want quantity, quantity, quantity!

If you had the opportunity to do some scouting ahead of time and found some fish, go there. If not, boat docks, fallen trees, or other large objects that cast a ton of shade are great places to start. While not every boat dock holds larger gamefish, it's rare to find one that doesn't have panfish holding tight.

When fishing docks take care not to damage another person's property, such as a boat the dock itself. I wouldn't recommend letting children learn how to cast near something they could break. Remember, you're setting an example for your kids, so set a respectful one.

If fishing a dock that you don't own, do ensure its owners aren't currently using it. While you probably aren't doing anything illegal (they usually don't own the water, no matter how much they think they do) it's just impolite to start fishing right next to someone who is trying to enjoy their backyard. This also sets you up for an altercation that can be embarrassing and potentially dangerous (after all, if a person has the gall to start screaming at a parent fishing with their kid, who knows what else they might do).

On the other hand, if you ever find yourself owning lakefront property, just remember that getting upset that people are fishing near your dock is like buying a house next to a school and then complaining about all the bells. There's no need to yell or make a scene. Always remember that it's just as awkward for the fisherman as it is for you, so simply hanging out nearby is usually enough to get all but the least polite angler to move on.

Fishing tends to be best in low light conditions, meaning dawn and dusk. If possible, try to take advantage of this. You want to try and target fish that are actively feeding and aggressive to enhance your odds of a strike or two. This isn't always the easiest thing to accomplish with young children as getting them up, fed, brushed, and ready for the day can feel a bit like moving the president, but the results are worth it.

If you must go during high noon, it's not the end of the world. Just try to find some shady spots where fish can shelter from the sun. Panfish will fight each other over worm scraps all day if you find them. Just poke around and look for their bubbles – you'll have action soon enough.

8 – PRIME FISHING LOCATIONS

You can't just walk up to any body of water, start casting your lure at the first place you stop and expect to be successful. Sure, it could work, but you're much more likely to catch a fish if you cast near habitat that might support them. In this chapter, we'll try to break that down a bit so that you can up your chances of catching fish quickly.

The first step is to realize that lakes, ponds, and rivers aren't that much different than land-based habitats. Look at any field or even your own backyard. There are probably some areas that the squirrels or deer favor more than others, and a few spots where you rarely see them. The same concept applies to fish. If you wanted to find a squirrel in your yard, you'd probably look near a tree. If you wanted to find a fish, you'd probably look for some weeds or other cover.

Structure vs. Cover

If you've spent any time at all around fishermen, or watching fishing programs on the television, you've heard plenty of people talk about "structure" and "cover." Though they might sound similar, they describe different elements of the fish's habitat. Understanding both is important to narrowing down a body of water and learning where you're likely to encounter fish.

Structure refers to the underwater topography of the lake. Most waterways aren't like swimming pools in that they don't all look like bowls where the shallows are confined to the edges, with the water getting progressively deeper as you move towards the middle. You'll find instead that most ponds, lakes, reservoirs, and rivers look an awful lot like the countryside around them. There will be sunken hills and valleys here and there, points, ridges, trenches, humps and islands all over the place.

All these features are structure, and fish will relate to them. Structure often works as underwater highways and fish will use it as landmarks as they move about their seasonal patterns. Structure can also be used to set up ambush points, especially in areas with current. Larger fish will often hold tight to the structure facing into the current, waiting for a meal to be swept within reach. Even without current, the natural corner or depression that structure creates can set up a prime ambush location.

Cover is a bit different than structure. While it can also provide good ambush points, its primary purpose is to give fish (and their prey) a sense of security. Cover includes weeds, brush, docks, rocks, and other elements that provide hiding places, ambush points, or shade.

What you really want to find is good structure that also has good cover. Take two extended points, for example. Both lead into deep, cooler, water and eventually drop off, but one is relatively barren and flat while the other is littered with jagged rocks and weeds. Fish will nearly always prefer the latter, even if both are identical in every other way.

Fancy electronics make finding structure and cover very easy, but if you don't have these, you can at least make an educated guess at what the bottom of a lake looks like by looking at the shore. The slope of the shoreline is usually a pretty good indicator of what the slope of the seabed will look like, at least at first. It would be very unusual for a gentle, flat field to suddenly plunge 20 feet at the waterline. Likewise, it would be odd to see cliffs at the seashore suddenly break into a flat and barren surface just under the water. While I suppose there are exceptions to every rule, it's far more likely that the gentle field is going to turn into a shallow bay, and the cliffs likely have deep water right next to them.

You can also get a pretty good idea of what sort of cover is under the waves, at least when it comes to rocks. If you see many large boulders on shore, chances are there are a few submerged not far from them. Likewise, riprap or even smaller stones tend to continue a bit into the sea. Just remember that if it looks manmade, it probably doesn't continue further than it needs to.

Although it probably won't be an immediate help, another thing you can do to understand structure and cover better is to take a walk around your favorite waterways in times of low water levels. While a drought will put a damper on many fishing trips, it can be a great opportunity to understand what the water looks like in your pond, to better rule out unproductive areas in future years. Even in normal times, a stroll around the lake just before winter can yield ample intelligence.

Another option (and a terrific one at that) is the satellite imagery available online through various mapping software. Some of this comes with historic imagery, and you can go back and find years with drought to see what was uncovered when the satellite passed over. For example, Lake Champlain had very low water levels in 2016, so photos taken at that time reveal many sunken features that you would never know existed. Try researching your local area's years of drought and then searching for satellite images from around that time. It would be an extremely productive use of a few hours.

Cuts & Creek Mouths

I've yet to find a cut or creek mouth that didn't hold fish. These are exceptionally important habitats and nurseries for several species and for good reason. There is usually a current or flow of fresh, clear water, vital nutrients, and lots of prey hanging near. Some of the largest fish that I have caught have come from a cut or the mouth of a creek, and some of the most consistent action has been found there as well.

Some of the best times to fish these areas are early in the spring and late in the fall. Creeks tend to flow out next to spawning bays and the deeper water around their mouths can be a good holding area for pre-spawn fish. Later in the year, certain baitfish like shad move shallow with some regularity as the water temperature cools, and larger fish follow them.

One of the best fishing holes I've ever found is a very small creek mouth leading from a pond to a small stream through a culvert. To access it from the pond, you'd have to cross a shallow spawning bay and enter the stream's mouth, which is totally covered by trees which lean into the water. There is a large amount of rip rap that forms a little hill before diving down into a depression right before the culvert. During the summer, that hill and most of the rest of the area is squarely above water, but each spring as the floods come the waters rise 2-3' and this creates the perfect ambush point for predators. They stack up on the lee side of the underwater hill and smash any prey that crosses it. It is not unusual to take 3-5 bass from 4-6lbs one cast after the other. The action stops after the waters recede, but it just goes to show how great one of these areas can be under the right conditions.

Predators love creek mouths and cuts because their prey does too. If there wasn't an ample supply of panfish that would frequent these waters, you'd never find the larger fish there. This makes them prime locations to take your kids, because they have the chance for a very large and exciting "bonus fish" while filling the livewell with their main panfish targets.

Docks

I talked quite a bit about docks in the last chapter as they are solid locations to take your kids fishing, and a great place to start your day. I'll try not to repeat what I said before but will add a few things for you to chew on.

The best dock is one you own, on a lake where you can chum with rabbit food. If you do this a few times a day for 2-3 days, your kids are going to have more fish to reel in than they can deal with. The chum will attract panfish of every size and sort, bowfin, bullhead, catfish, and strange, weird creatures you'll need to look up.

Unfortunately, not everyone has their own dock (though we can all dare to dream). This doesn't mean you can't fish someone else's (though as stated earlier, you'll want to be very respectful). Not all docks are created equal, however. The best docks tend to cast a lot of shade and have permanent pilings that fish can count on year by year to relate to. Floating docks can also be productive, but they tend to be taken out each year (at least in the north) and so they can take a while to attract fish. The biggest concern is how low the dock is to the actual water. If it's right against it, it's going to provide better cover and shade than one that is several feet above the waterline (unless, of course, it's wide enough that this doesn't matter). On the other hand, it's very challenging to skip a lure beneath a low dock, so there is always some give and take.

Points

Points are exactly what they sound like – pieces of structure that extend out from the shore and "point" towards the sea. They tend to be outstanding fishing spots, although they can be difficult to fish in poor weather because they tend to be much more exposed to the wind than the bays on either side.

Rocky points near spawning bays tend to hold a ton of bass early in the year, though you might need to poke around a bit to find the one they want. They also hold panfish, which makes them a good choice if you're following the maxim of quantity over quality. They, like creek mouths, are good places to find a "bonus fish" while you're targeting other species.

Identifying which part of the point will hold fish can be challenging at times, but if you're fishing with live bait such as nightcrawlers, you'll soon enough feel taps and zero in on this. I'd recommend that you generally start on whichever side is opposite the prevailing direction of the wind (the technical term would be the leeward side), as the point can provide a good ambush point and current break. Working your lure or bait towards the top of the point's hump and then down its backside is a good way to draw a strike.

Jetties

These are essentially man-made points. They'll hold panfish and bass and can be a good fishing spot with kids, especially since they often offer some of the best (or only) shore-access fishing around. The only issue to remember is that plenty of other people have this idea and so you'd better get out early before all the spots are taken.

Even better than one jetty are two jetties running towards each other with a channel in-between. This creates a situation where current can form when the wind is blowing, and fish will stack up to take advantage of this. I've watched more than a few fishing shows where the pros will just hover over these locations and catch fish one by one. Any time that you can find a situation where the fishing is fast and furious is a good time to have your kid with you.

If you're approaching a jetty from a boat, try to be mindful of the fact that the folks on shore can't exactly motor off to anywhere they choose. While you have every right to also fish these waters, try to be respectful and not ruin anyone's day. I tend to try and avoid fishing too close to families on the shore. For that matter, I extend the same courtesy to folks in rowboats and kayaks when I'm on my motorboat.

Bridge Pilings

These permanent structures hold fish year-round as they provide a current break, structure to relate to, and shade throughout the day. Fish will often hold tight to them and strike nightcrawlers or drop shots as they sink along the piling. Yellow perch and white perch seem particularly drawn to these areas, as do smallmouth bass in lakes that have them.

Like jetties, these tend to be popular spots, especially if one can fish from the bridge itself, so you might want to get there early. If you are in a boat and see some people on the actual bridge, move a short distance away and fish a different piling, or the other side of one. Remember, they have far less options than you.

Drop Offs & Pools

For various reasons, many fish favor drop offs. The structure might act as some sort of highway for them to relate to, or perhaps they just appreciate having access to deeper water nearby. The fancier trolling motors with GPS do a good job of patrolling along these structure breaks automatically, but you can usually tell where they are simply by observing the weed line.

Weeds in the lake aren't that much different than weeds in your garden. They tend to grow everywhere unless there's a good reason not to. Some of the common reasons that certain areas lack aquatic vegetation include a change in depth (some plants can only grow in water so deep), or bottom content (some plants require certain types of bottom composition to grow in). Knowing this, you can "read" a bay to an extent and figure out where the deeper pools or drop-offs are based on where the weeds aren't matted to the surface.

Pools are areas of deeper water surrounded by shallow water. Certain species prefer the cooler, deeper areas either for their change in temperature or, again, cover and concealment for striking out at unwary prey. You'll most commonly hear people referring to pools in rivers, but you can find them in lakes and ponds as well.

When fishing rivers or creeks, you'll tend to have better luck in the pools than in the neighboring shallows. These pools allow fish to get out of the current and ambush prey that is swept by in it. There only needs to be a foot or two in difference to draw in fish, and panfish are just as likely to favor this as larger species.

It can be challenging to find pools in rivers because many of the ones near your home might not allow for boat traffic. If you must look out from the shore, try to find any area where it figures that water would erode or cut into the bottom. Generally, this is going to be the outside bends of the river, as this is where the bottom is exposed to the full force of the current.

Spawning Bays & Grassy Flats

Shallow bays are a great place to find panfish and larger "bonus fish" throughout the year, but especially in the spring. As discussed in Chapter 6, panfish such as bluegills will crowd around largemouth bass beds trying to pick off their eggs and fry. This stacks the smaller fish and makes it very easy to target them with your kids during the spawn.

These areas continue to hold fish during the summer. The biggest challenge when fishing with your children will be the weeds, as many of these shallow bays fill up with them. There can still be good action for panfish and others in the little holes and pockets, but it can be tough for kids to cast to these accurately, or to have the patience to let their bait lie there long enough for a fish to strike. Reeling in before they have a bite is a good way to get snagged on weeds.

It's not all that much better when the fish does bite, because the first thing they're going to do is dash for the nearest clump of weeds to try and escape. You'll need to keep a firm eye on the fish and keep plenty of tension on them while you're waiting for your kid to scramble over and take the rod.

For these reasons, these spawning bays can be somewhat challenging to take kids into later in the year and you might do better chasing white perch or other panfish species that can be found easily enough in deeper water near pilings or rocky points.

Grassy flats can be spawning bays or considerably larger areas of relatively uniform depth, lined with weeds or "grass." When your kids are old enough to cast decently (or if you've decided to give trolling a try during lunch), grassy flats can make for some good fun, especially in lakes that hold pickerel and northern pike. If you can find flats that are approximately 8 – 12' deep and can find weeds that are about 2' below the surface of the water, burning spinnerbaits over them (either by hand or with the trolling motor) can call up some truly giant fish.

The action probably won't be as good as a school of panfish would provide, but if your kids are past the age where they absolutely need a bite every 30 seconds, this can be a great option to start searching for some larger fish to tug their line and heartstrings.

The Northwest Corner

In the northern hemisphere, the northwest corner of any bay is going to warm up the fastest each spring. This is because it's exposed to the sun longer given its relation to the earth. It's worth keeping this in mind very early in the year as you'll often find the more active fish in this corner because the water temperatures can be a few degrees higher, which can make all the difference.

If you can happen to find a northwest corner that is also a shallow spawning flat that is near deeper water and a creek mouth, you've struck gold. There is a reason that so many bass boats stack up right next to Fort Ticonderoga on Lake Champlain. It checks all those boxes. It's a northwest bay with shallow spawning flats situated right between the La Chute River and the channel drop off. For these reasons, plenty of professionals over the years have gambled driving all the way from Plattsburgh in a tournament. The drive there and back can take well over an hour each way, so over the course of 3-4 days it more or less amounts to "spotting" the competition an entire day of fishing, reckoning that with spots like this, you don't need the extra time.

Cribs, Christmas Trees, and Underwater Rock Piles

I was tempted to call this section "honey holes" as that's what they tend to amount to, but I wanted to be a bit more descriptive. Basically, there are certain areas where people have sunk objects to draw in fish. These can take the form of cribs, a bunch of rocks, Christmas trees, or even commercial fish attractors.

People tend to deploy these in the dead of night when no one is looking, and never tell a soul. You'll suspect that there's something out there soon enough when you start seeing the same old boats hanging around random spots mid-lake. A pass by these with your sonar deployed can often unveil some goodies.

To understand why these work, conduct an experiment the next time you're swimming in a natural lake. Grab a bunch of stones and put them in a pile. See how quickly the panfish stack up next to them. Sometimes you'll see them within minutes, especially if you do this near some form of structure that they favor.

The same concept applies to larger, man-deployed cover. Some professional bass tournaments have even been won by anglers who have made their own honey holes doing this, though doing so tends to stir the pot up well and causes a lot of controversy.

The Effect of Water Temperature

Water temperature can drastically alter a fish's behavior, so a good thermometer is a very important tool. Luckily, they are inexpensive and thus well within the reach of anyone on foot or in a boat. Most fish finders come with one pre-installed, but if you're off hiking with the kids in tow, you can pick a handheld surface temperature reader up to help you along.

These are particularly important early and late in the year when fish will really gravitate to certain areas based on water temp. Lake Champlain flooded again in 2019, which was good in that it opened considerable areas to explore yet challenging in that certain areas (particularly around creek mouths) weren't as productive as usual.

I believe the reason for this was the water temperature. I was fishing a bay near one creek and found that the temperatures near its mouth were 5 to 7 degrees cooler than the surrounding water. It didn't matter that this was the northwest bay because any effect the southern sun had on the water temps was nullified by the influx of cold runoff from the nearby creek. It wasn't until I moved away from this area, back into spots that usually don't produce as well (but which now held warmer water), that the fish started striking.

It is worth noting, however, that water temps can stabilize from such situations very quickly. A few days later in the week, the temperatures rose considerably, and I started landing good fish in their traditional habitat along the northwest corner.

As seen in Chapter 6, different species have their preferred temperature ranges, so if you are fishing with older kids or looking for a good "bonus fish" for the younger ones, it would make sense to pay attention to this and seek appropriate water temps to give your family the best chance of hooking into one.

The Effect of Weather

If you're reading this before you head off on vacation, you're probably checking the weather with concern at the hint of any clouds or rain. We all want our vacations to be sunny and beautiful. From a fishing perspective, however, clouds and rain aren't the end of the world. In fact, they can often help the fishing as cloudy skies reduce the amount of light that penetrates the water, meaning that fish can be more active.

Inbound storms have a way of stirring up nature to the extent that some of the best fishing I've ever experienced was just before a storm hit. There are several scientific reasons why that are beyond the scope of this work but trust me – if thunderclouds are on the horizon, the fishing picks up.

It's very similar to that scene in *Caddyshack* where the golfer is having the best game of his life. Just be careful that it's not *too* similar (spoiler alert: golfing in a lightning storm is a dumb idea. Almost as dumb as fishing in a lightning storm). Obviously, when you have your children you need to be extra careful about storms as they aren't going to be able to run off the boat as quickly as you, so don't wait until the last second to get home.

While fishing can be great before the front moves in, it generally slows down afterwards. This is what people refer to as "post-frontal conditions." When the skies are completely blue after the passing of a storm, the fishing can be brutal. It doesn't seem to affect panfish (or at least the spritely smaller ones) quite as much as large gamefish, so you still have a pretty good chance of having a nice time with your kids, but if you're fishing with older ones and targeting larger species you might have some trouble. In general, you'll want to slow down your presentations and put your lure right in front of the fish's face. Drop shots and plastic worms are great tools for these tough days.

A Word of Warning

Take care not to put too much stock into what worked last year, or even what "should" work this trip. This is a hard trap not to fall into, but it's so important and even more so when you're taking your children out and trying to put them on fish. If a rocky point was just lighting it up for you last year and you find that nothing is working there now, consider that perhaps the fish have spawned earlier and move into bays. Likewise, if those bays were on fire but now there's nothing, try the points. Don't let your history with an area force your hand and make you stick with unproductive water or presentations with kids in the boat.

The same goes for the types of lures you're throwing, or how you present them. You always want to let the fish tell you what they want, rather than trying to impose your will on them.

9 – PURCHASING A BOAT

There will come a time when you will wish that you had a boat, and that time will be about twenty minutes after you've started fishing from the bank. You're going to get fed up with how much of the shoreline is impossible for you to reach, much less your kids, and you'll think the fish are taunting you as they jump repeatedly *just* out of reach of your best cast. You're going to read plenty of books and watch plenty of videos about covering water and despair a bit that you really can't do that (at least effectively, and at least with kids). You might pout a bit.

Hopefully, your kid hooks a nice bluegill just as you are feeling bad for yourself and you stop wallowing in your self-pity long enough to concentrate on their smile for a bit, but soon enough the feeling will return, and I'm not going to try and convince you to ignore it. You are a fisherman or fisherwoman, and so are your children. Regardless of what anyone else says, and regardless of how many fish you can catch from shore, yes, you need a boat!

Well, that's just not in the cards for everyone – at least not yet. But then again, it's nice to have a goal, and this goal isn't as insurmountable as you might imagine. Online tag sales and the like are flooded with small craft in the $200-$1,000 range. Look hard enough and you might even find someone willing to give one away for free, if only you'll pick it up.

You don't need something with all the bells and whistles, especially if you're just starting out. You do need something reasonably stable for young kids, as they don't listen any better to "stop rocking the boat! You're going to tip us over!" as they do to "stop kicking the walls!

You're going to wake your sister up!"

*There are few sights more glorious than your own boat
waiting for you at the dock.*

Storing the Boat

The first consideration of course is whether you have anywhere to park this boat. This is going to determine what type of boat you can purchase, if any.

If you don't own or rent a home, this can be challenging as many condos and apartments have no space for a boat or don't allow their storage. Many people consider boats unsightly, so you might have trouble convincing friends or family to let you store it at their home if you can't keep it at your own.

You could pay for storage, either at a marina or by renting a garage or storage locker somewhere, but you'd better be clear on why you're in the apartment or condo in the first place – is it by choice or necessity? If you just hate cutting grass and shoveling snow and prefer the condo lifestyle but have disposable income, then no harm no foul in paying for some storage. On the other hand, if you're there because you're just starting out, then don't let this (or any other) hobby set you back further. Have a solid foundation and a secure life for your kids before you go and set yourself back spending money on a toy (even if it's an awesome one).

If you do own a home, is there a homeowners' association? Do they have bylaws limiting where boats can be stored? Does it have to be in your backyard, or garage? How large of a boat can you fit there?

If you're planning on storing your boat on your property, do you have somewhere level to put it? This isn't critical – my driveway is slanted, and a good set of wheel chocks keeps my boat firmly in place – but it's very, very preferable to store any type of trailered boat on level land. The reason you want to do this if possible is because it's a pain in the butt to connect a trailer to your vehicle's trailer hitch on a hill, because you must back up your vehicle precisely.

On level ground, with smaller boats and single-axel trailers at least, you can back your vehicle close and then actually move the trailer by hand if you were off a few inches. If you try to do this on a hill, either your trailer tongue is going to punch a hole through the back of your truck, your boat's motor will wind up in your living room, or you are going to be the mushy filling of a boat-truck sandwich.

Another consideration when parking on a hill is that you'll need to ensure the stern (rear) of your boat is facing downhill. If you don't, then any water that gets in will stay in the bilge and cause all your equipment to develop mold. This might mean that you need to pull your boat in rather than back it, which isn't traditional but is certainly better than a ruined boat.

It's not the end of the world if you have to park it on a slight hill, but it's something to consider when you're looking for a boat because you might find a model that has a swing-away trailer tongue and can fit in your garage. The scenarios above would be solid reasons to pursue that option if it was the only way to avoid leaving the boat on a slant.

Inflatables

If you live in an apartment and have nowhere to put a boat, your options are going to be very limited. Basically, you'll need something that you can fit inside your rental. Since the scope of this book exclusively deals with fishing with your children, we can throw out single-person small craft like kayaks or tube floats. Thus, your only real option for getting your kids out on the water is an inflatable raft of some kind.

These are not ideal for fishing by yourself or with kids, but you make the best of what life deals you. Inflatables are serviceable at least and will get you out on the water. They work well for smaller ponds or coves where you wouldn't expect much wind or waves, so they are fine for catching panfish. They are also the lightest option out there, so you might find yourself taking some "me time" trips out to a few ponds.

They come in different sizes and some are rated for as many as five people, so it's possible to get your family out on one of these. When you factor in the need to fit at least some fishing gear, bigger is going to be better.

These can be had for about $20 at your local big box store, though I wouldn't recommend going that low. You get what you pay for and the less expensive options are going to have thinner rubber that is more likely to puncture. Remember, you're using this for fishing with small children and hooks! Thin rubber is a bad, bad idea! You'll also find that the cheaper the price, the flimsier these craft tend to be, which means they'll be less stable and enjoyable in general. Let's face it – you're not buying one of these things for any other reason than it's the only boat you can fit where you live, so invest a little bit in it if you can. You can still have nice things in a small space!

If you're going the inflatable route, there are a few accessories you'll want to consider. An anchor is going to be indispensable, because that raft is so light weight it will be tossed around by any wind. Further, you're going to want to have some mechanical means of inflating your raft, because you're going to get sick of trying to blow it up by mouth very quickly. A bicycle pump is an improvement, but an automatic pump that plugs into your car is the best. Failing to bring one of these along is going to delay your excursion, to say the least.

Some people build removable floorboards for their rafts. ½ Inch plywood works well and can be carpeted if desired. This will give the craft a little stability and give you a little piece of mind with the kids as you won't feel like you're fishing on an air mattress. There's also the factor that at least one part of the craft will be hook-proof.

If you do decide to build your own floorboards, there are plenty of blog posts out there that can help, with detailed photographs and instructions. I'd recommend this option if you go the inflatable route. It's a pretty straight-forward DIY job that will make a huge difference out on the water, especially with kids in the raft.

While an inflatable probably isn't your dream boat, it's just as capable as any other watercraft of putting a huge smile on your kid's face. Even just paddling to the far side of a pond is a grand adventure for kids, and this is one boat you can trust them with when they're pretty young, assuming you can trust them to wear their life jacket and they know how to swim.

Canoes & Gheenoes

The next step up from an inflatable raft would probably be a canoe. These can be hung from a garage wall or ceiling and cartopped to the lake, which makes them plausible for condo dwellers who aren't allowed to own trailers. They are also relatively inexpensive, with brand new models available from sporting goods stores for less than $500, and no shortage of people looking to get rid of them in the classifieds.

A canoe won't puncture and sink the first time your child snags a hook into it, but they can be unstable which makes them a precarious option with young children. Certainly, your kids need to be old enough to know how to listen and sit down. You don't want them standing up, rocking the canoe back and forth, and running all around. Even if they "forget," as long as you're paying attention, you should be able to keep the craft righted by shifting your own weight if your kids get a bit excited, but if you're in the middle of untangling a knot and your attention is diverted, you could get wet.

There are products called canoe stabilizers which can be bought or built that reduce the risk of tipping, and they're a wise investment for the parent angler. They're basically little outriggers that attach to the sides of the canoe and extend outward. If the canoe starts to tip to one side, the outrigger is forced into the water, which stabilizes the craft.

There is a canoe-like watercraft called a gheenoe that you might want to explore. I own one and love it. They have a unique hull design that makes them far more stable than normal canoes. While they are substantially more expensive than your average canoe, they make an excellent choice for families because of their stability. There are several different rigging options including additional seats, storage, and even a livewell. Of course, the more options you load up on it, the less likely you're storing this from your garage ceiling or wall. In fact, the larger models require a trailer, though the benefit is they can also accept a good-sized outboard engine.

If interested, you should take a look at the different types on www.gheenoe.net, as well as www.customgheenoe.com, or watch some videos by their owners showing off the stability. One problem you may find is that gheenoes are somewhat of a regional boat. It's much easier to find a dealer or a used one in Florida than New England. I live in New England and had to travel three states away to purchase mine. The seller was the only one for hundreds of miles around and knew this. I had zero bargaining power and the only discount I could negotiate was a consideration for the gas I'd pay to pick it up. Unless you live in the southeast, you will likely be faced with the same position.

While you will likely pay asking price, it's still worth going through a dealer if you can, because these boats are highly customizable from the factory to suit your every need. While I wouldn't recommend breaking the bank on one as you'd be challenged to get your money back, you could at least consider different seating options and deck layouts. For example, mine has a raised casting deck in the front and rear with a large storage box in the center. As I wanted to bring two kids at some point, having three spots where each of us could stand or sit was important to me. Others favor getting rid of the center box as the boat is even more stable if you're standing in the main cabin.

I spent many years researching small watercraft before purchasing my gheenoe to compliment my Lund and am pleased with the purchase. It was important to me that I could stand while fishing, and I wanted something stable enough that I could take a small child in who isn't always the best listener, or most relaxed. I also wanted something small enough that I could drag it in and out of the water myself in undeveloped areas, though these do push the limit there as they weigh in at well over 100 pounds.

Rowboats & Johnboats

These craft look like traditional boats but tend to be very bare bones. Some are light enough to cartop while others are going to require a trailer. With two adults it's usually possible to carry them a short distance, which means you can launch them just about anywhere. If you're going alone with your kids, you might need a ramp, or at least a parking space close enough where you can reasonably drag the boat to the water by yourself.

These small craft tend to be more stable than canoes because they have a wider beam. They can often carry more people and gear, which makes them a better option if you have a few kids to take out. Most don't come equipped with a livewell, though you can purchase one as a kit.

It can be very inexpensive to get into one of these boats, as it seems like they're a dime and dozen in the classified ads. There are many sitting out in someone's shed or barn collecting dust that people are willing to get rid of for a few hundred dollars. They're simple boats to inspect on your own as they don't have many hidden compartments or things that can go wrong. You could simply ask the seller for a hose and fill them with water to see if they have any leaks and call it a day. Even if there are leaks, some liberal use of an epoxy can usually fix them, and for a few hundred dollars, who cares if it looks a little crazy.

If you enjoy projects, you can customize these hulls quite a bit. There is a website, www.tinboats.net, that has a robust forums section full of people who have taken old and rusting beat up rowboats and johnboats and turned them into gorgeous, carpeted fishing machines. I've seen projects with a working livewell, raised casting decks, in-floor rod storage, and much, much more. This could be a fun project with your kids, if they're into stuff like that.

Crappie Boats

I'd classify the boat I grew up on as a crappie, or panfish boat. Note that this is named after the fish and is not a statement of quality—that little boat did just fine for my dad and three kids over 20 years!

These are basically smaller motorboats, generally aluminum, and shaped somewhat like a bass boat. They tend to be economical as they are less expensive to purchase, maintain, and operate. They do just fine on most lakes although you're going to want to pick your days and not head out in the worst weather.

Dad used to have a 15' model with three seat bases in a row, no rod storage to speak of, and a little 28 horsepower Evinrude motor to putt us around Lake Champlain. We caught thousands of fish out of that boat and it was one he was able to pay cash for. That's a good machine in my mind.

When looking at a boat in this style, I would recommend trying to find one with as much floor space as possible. Although dad's boat did the trick, its seats were on giant boxes which left very little room for anything in the boat. The boxes were for storage but of course this meant that something had to fit in the box to be stored there. It wasn't ideal and I would have preferred some pedestal bases so I would have had more room. Further, more floor space often means that the boat has a wider beam, which is worth every penny when taking your children out.

One of the best things about this style of boat is that it's hard for the day to be ruined in one. If the main motor won't start, the boat is small enough that your trolling motor can take you far and wide (also a benefit in electric only lakes). If you find that you forgot to charge the trolling motor, paddling is still an option (you will curse at yourself, but you can still put your kids on fish with a little sweat). Even if you forgot the paddle, if you have a rope, you theoretically could get in the water and play the role of tugboat. If your engine won't start, your batteries aren't charged, and you forgot the paddle and the rope, well, maybe this just isn't for you.

Bass Boats

If you really enjoy fishing, you probably dream of one day owning a bass boat. They are sleek, sexy, and glamorous. They can be equipped with the latest technology and are bass catching machines. Even so, I'd suggest holding off on buying one until your kids are older as bass boats aren't ideal for younger children or larger families.

To start, bass boats can't really fit as many people (at least as comfortably) as different styles, like multi-species and pontoon boats discussed below. They generally have three seats in a line and if you want to put more people in them, they need to sit on the floor somewhere.

Bass boats also have very low gunnels as their floors tend to be flush with their sides. You really fish "on" a bass boat as opposed to "in" one. The implications for young children should be obvious – they can fall out much more easily. Throw in some waves or a large boat wake and you could have a dangerous situation.

There's also the problem of speed. Bass boats are like little sports cars in that most can hit at least 50-60 mph, and many are capable of speeds of 70-80 mph or greater. It should go without saying that you shouldn't be going anywhere near this fast with your kids in the boat, but sometimes things can get the better of you. Higher speeds increase the risk of collision with submerged objects, other boats, or animals (yes, you can hit a deer in the lake just as you can hit one on the road). These boats are also prone to losing control, sometimes spectacularly, when the driver doesn't know what they're doing.

While I certainly don't recommend this style for younger children, they are undoubtedly the best type of boat if you're going to enter bass fishing tournaments (you won't find a professional bass angler fishing anything else), so once your children get older, you might consider transitioning to one of these, especially if your kids want to take a serious run at a college bass fishing scholarship.

Bass boats can operate in extremely shallow water, and their lower sides catch less wind, making them easier to position appropriately for the next cast. These same low sides make certain lure presentations, such as pitching, significantly easier. It is also less difficult to land fish, as you're closer to the water.

They can be rigged with a variety of electronics that make life much better. Shallow water anchors are a tremendous, game-changing invention, as are some of the more advanced sonar units on the market these days. All of this combines to help people catch more fish.

This could potentially pay off for your kids in a big way. As of 2019, several high schools and colleges have fishing teams, with some of the latter even awarding scholarships for exceptional young anglers. There are college tournaments with additional scholarship prize money to be won, and these can be a great way for your kids to either attempt to launch a career doing something they love, or at least get very valuable experience in marketing that they can use in an interview someday.

If fishing becomes one of your child's main sports, it wouldn't be the worst idea to investigate one of these craft eventually – just hold off while they're young unless you're primarily buying this for you.

Multi-Species Boats

Also called "walleye boats," a multi-species, deep-v vessel is ideal for fishing with children. It is what I own and recommend, as it has made taking my kids and their friends out on the water a breeze.

These boats have high gunnels which is peace of mind for a parent. I can focus on a tangle or unhooking a fish for a few moments without worrying about my son falling overboard. If there's a rogue wave or a particularly rude boater who throws up a large wake near me, I know we'll be safe.

I've been in very rough seas on Lake Champlain and even caught directly in a microburst (thankfully without the kids) and lived to tell the tale. While I wouldn't recommend traveling in poor weather, sometimes fate turns on you, so it's nice to have a boat that gives you confidence that you'll make it home alive.

My boat has a walk-through windshield, which I am grateful for every time it shields me from some water spray while underway. This same windshield makes the ride considerably warmer in cold weather because it will shield you from most of the wind, but if it's still too cold for my son, he'll just tuck himself in on the floor behind the passenger console and find even more shelter.

Another major safety enhancement with these boats is that they can be rigged with kicker motors. These are smaller than your main outboard, but also gas powered. If something goes wrong with the big motor, the kicker can get you safely back home (albeit slowly). Combined with a trolling motor, you now have a triple redundancy. If something were to happen while you were taking your kids out on a larger lake or reservoir, this could prove vital.

Multi-species boats don't have as shallow of a draft as bass boats so they can't get into as shallow of water, which is a disadvantage, but they make up for this in being much more practical for other fishing techniques such as trolling. Most bass tournaments prohibit trolling and accordingly you won't find many accessories designed to help anglers troll from bass boats. This is not the case with the multi-species boat, so there are plenty of downriggers, rod holders, and other accessories that can be inexpensively had for your multispecies boat. This opens the lake to you and your kids, and regardless of the available species in your area, you're able to target them.

Speaking of accessing different areas, these boats are plausible options for taking out in the ocean (though you wouldn't want to go very far). It's common in New England and elsewhere to see boats of this style cruising the coastal waters looking for species beyond the scope of this book. While there's nothing that says a bass boat can't also do this (Some companies build intercoastal models of bass boats for this exact purpose), all the issues you'd encounter with a big lake are only exacerbated once out to sea, and the triple redundancy motor system becomes all the more important.

Most of these boats have a very wide beam and open floor plans, especially if you remove a few of the seats. Many of them come with flip-up "jump seats" of sorts towards the back, which can fold down to become a casting deck, or flipped up for extra passengers. When folded down, they also make a great "tanning platform" for your wife, which is a good way to help sell her on the idea of a boat in the first place.

One nice option that you'll tend to find in these boats is partial or complete vinyl flooring. My boat has this, and I love it as it's significantly easier to keep clean than carpet. My son is an expert at knocking over worm coolers and getting the dirt everywhere. The vinyl flooring makes cleanup very easy. If the dirt is dry, I simply vacuum it up. If wet, I just take out a brush and a hose and spray the boat down.

Vinyl does get hotter than carpet, which makes it difficult on small knees and dogs, and is one reason that some people elect the partial option. A boat with a partial vinyl floor has carpet in the bow and aft casting decks, but vinyl in the main floor. As this is where everyone is sitting, children tend to fish from, and the mess is likely to occur, it's a very practical option.

If you go with this partial vinyl floor plan, many manufactures offer a snap-in carpet option which allows you to have the best of both worlds. Snap in the carpet on hot days and take it out when you're expecting your kids to knock the worms all over. You also might opt for a full vinyl floor (including both casting decks) but elect the snap-in carpet for the main floor in case you want a place where your kids can play on the ground, or the dog can lay down without overheating.

While certainly a dedicated fishing boat, this style also does well for water sports like pulling tubes. Many come with bases to install a ski pylon, and most have sturdy boarding ladders for people to climb back aboard after they're done messing around and want to get back to fishing.

All in all, the multi-species boat is a great choice for a family. While some of them can run as much or more than a bass boat, they don't have to. There are plenty of entry level models in the 16' to 17' range that can be quite affordable, and in the north at least, there's no shortage of used models. If you're looking for one, or have any questions about the style in general, I recommend visiting the boat forums over at www.walleyecentral.com. There are several helpful folks over there who are more than willing to share their knowledge and opinions. This same website also has a well-used classifieds section where you can find many used boats in this style.

Fish & Ski Boats

These boats very much resemble multi-species boats (in fact, some are marketed as slight variations of them) but they are geared more towards water sports than fishing. They can be a very good option for a family, especially if not everyone in it (cough, cough, your significant other) is as excited about fishing as you and the kids.

Often, they'll have a place to put water skies, and they'll usually come equipped with a base to place a ski pylon for dragging water-skiers or pulling tubes. They tend to be rated for more people than a similar multi-species boat, which can be helpful for larger families or taking the kids' friends out. Many have cushions in the bow which are removable but are a nice addition for lounging around in the sun.

If you decide to go the fish & ski route but are still serious about fishing, I would recommend looking for a brand that specializes in fishing boats but offers a few fish & ski models as well. The reason you want this is these manufacturers tend to build their fish & ski models with much the same fishing options as the dedicated multi-species boats.

If you go for a brand that is primarily interested in cruising, it can be challenging to find one that even has a dedicated place for a bow mount trolling motor. Often, the bow will not have a raised casting deck, or even a seat base. If you look at them, you'll see what I mean – they clearly weren't designed for someone to stand up front and fish from all day. Rather, their bow is likely cushioned for idle lounging.

Unless fishing is going to be a very minor use for this boat, I really wouldn't recommend purchasing a boat primarily designed for cruising. You're much better off getting one that is designed for the best of both worlds because if you don't, many of the headaches that come with fishing (primarily focused on boat control) are going to be exacerbated by a model not designed for the task.

Pontoon Boats

These are enormous boats and can be enormous fun. While they're essentially giant sails and thus very difficult to control and position for precise fishing presentations, they really aren't designed so much for drifting a bank as they are for weighing anchor and soaking some lines while grilling up a few burgers and listening to some tunes.

They can be ideal boats for grandparents or other adults who anticipate bringing a gaggle of children aboard as you can fit many people safely and legally. There's so much room on some models that kids could practically play tag on them if you let them.

They make great swim platforms and it's perfectly possible to have half the family jumping into the water on one side while a few others are catching panfish on the other.

Despite their size, they can be quite fast – certainly fast enough to pull tubes or water skiers with the appropriate motor. I wouldn't go so far as to call them "nimble," however, so if water skiing is a major joy for you, you might consider one of the fish and ski models discussed above.

A significant disadvantage is that you need a ton of space to store them, and they tend to require larger vehicles to tow them safely. You'll also be limited as to where you can launch them given their width, and they can be difficult to launch alone (although, in fairness, if you're buying one of these boats, the chances of *being* alone are slim to none). Many times, you'll find people with lake houses and pontoon boats just leave their boat in the water the entire year because of these factors.

As stated above, they are a pain to control in the wind and aren't likely to produce many tournament victories, but if you're looking for a great boat to take your entire family and all their friends out for a fun day, it would be hard to find a better option.

Glass vs. Tin

You won't be very long into your boat research when you stumble across a debate on the forums over what is better, glass or tin.

Glass refers to fiberglass boats. They tend to be more expensive, but also provide drier, and arguably safer rides because they are heavier and thus handle rough seas and windy days better than aluminum boats. This increased weight means that you'll pay more at the pump for the boat itself as well as its tow vehicle.

Tin boats are made of aluminum which makes them less expensive and lighter than their glass cousins. This makes them easier for one person to launch, and generally less expensive to operate as it takes less gas to propel them, and a smaller vehicle to tow them. Most mid-sized SUVs can pull a moderately-sized aluminum boat without any issues.

If you go with a tin boat, the next thing to decide will be rivets vs. welds. Both sides have their proponents and there are quality boats to be purchased with either design. If you take care of your stuff and purchase from a quality manufacturer with a solid warranty, you can't go wrong either way. Even so, I prefer rivets because if one breaks, I can fix the leak with some epoxy. It might not look pretty, but it's quick and effective. I don't want to think of how many cans of epoxy it would take to fix a burst weld.

To illustrate the point, I once had an older, riveted boat that was pretty banged up. I took some waves much harder than I should have and quickly found to my dismay that the boat was slowly sinking. I pulled it out of the water and was able to isolate the source of the leak. It wasn't a rivet, but the intake for the livewell system, which had broken clean off, leaving an inch-diameter hole directly in the bottom of the boat!

A hole that large directly in the bottom of a boat should ruin a vacation, but I was able to find a large plastic plumbing screw that was approximately the correct size, and then epoxy it in place. It looked awful, but the boat floated for years after.

You could easily do the same thing if a rivet or two, or three, or twenty failed and started to leak. My father did just that with his boat because he couldn't figure out where it was leaking. His solution was simple: just slap some epoxy on every rivet! Again, it wasn't going to win any beauty pageants, but it was effective.

Should You Buy a Used Boat?

Ok, so I've convinced you that you need a boat, and now your significant other hates me. Still, you've managed to convince them of the necessity and you're looking around for something that will work for your family. It's possible you've visited a showroom, and probable that you've wanted to throw up a little when you looked at the price of the new boat stickers. I'm with you on that – they are ridiculous and only getting worse year by year!

This of course brings you to look at used boats, but you have that nagging doubt about them. You probably aren't as comfortable examining a used boat as you would be looking for flaws in a used car, as this is your first rodeo. You might even ask yourself if it's safe to buy a used one, or if you should bite the bullet and buy new.

If it's your first boat, you're better off buying used, simply because you're probably going to do something stupid and damage it. I'm not trying to be pessimistic or offensive, but it's just the way things work. Just think back to your first car and all the dumb things you did with that. Do you really think you'll do better with something you use once a week at best?

Buying used also means that you don't take as much, if any, of a hit with depreciation, which is a big deal if you ever need to get out from under the boat. There are a lot of hidden expenses with boat ownership and sometimes people bite off more than they can chew. I'd like to help you avoid that if possible.

You'll find you have some options for buying used. There's the private market and used boat sales at dealerships. You're going to pay a premium at the dealership but it's not a bad idea as sometimes they'll warranty the boat for a short period, and a good dealer at least should be pretty friendly and helpful if something goes wrong, and you politely explain the issue (they don't want you flooding the internet with horror stories about them, after all). The fishing and boating marketplace relies heavily on word of mouth and relationship building, so you're less likely to find someone out to put the screws to you, especially in the age of social media.

That doesn't mean that things can't go wrong. Some of these boats they're selling are very old and come "as is" with no warranty. If the seller is up front about that, it's hard to fault them if there is an issue with the boat. It is on you to come armed with a bit of knowledge about how to look for at least the obvious issues, and it would behoove you to bring along someone more experienced if you're not confident you can do this. There are also several videos out there by marine mechanics and surveyors that can assist you with this. I'll give you some basic tips, but when you're talking about a purchase this large, research several sources.

At the very least, you'll want to make sure you cover the basics. Does the boat look like it has generally been taken care of, or does it look beat to hell? You can't always judge a book by its cover, but a prior owner who took the time to maintain the exterior of a boat probably also did what he or she could to maintain the mechanicals.

When walking around on the boat, can you feel any weak spots in the floor? Repairing a floor is expensive, and a weak floor can indicate that the transom may also be compromised—after all, if one area of marine plywood is failing, why wouldn't the other?

The transom is the back of the boat where the motor hangs from. While more and more companies are going to composite fiberglass transoms that won't rot, the transoms for many older boats are made of wood. If properly manufactured and maintained, these can last for decades, but if they fail it's a very labor-intensive and costly process to replace them.

To spot a bad transom, take your hand and apply some pressure to the outboard. Does the transom flex? How substantially? If it's flexing a lot, that could be an issue. You also might notice some stress cracks along corners or other areas where the transom meets the sides and bottom of the boat, which is another indicator that there is an issue. If you don't see either of these, that doesn't mean it's fine, but at least it probably isn't terminal.

Some other ways to check for a bad transom include taking a rubber mallet and gently tapping all around it. You're trying to notice a change in sound from a crisp return into a dull one (go try pounding on a fresh piece of plywood compared to a rotting one to hear the difference). You can also take a screw, wire coat hanger, or other similar object and poking around in a screw hole for an uninstalled transducer mount, trying to see if the wood inside feels mushy or starts to leak.

All these steps probably seem a bit little overkill, but you can easily be looking at a few thousand-dollar repair if the transom is bad, so spend some time looking it over as best you can.

Once you determine that the transom seems to be in pretty good shape, it's time to inspect the motor. If you're serious about the boat, it might make sense to hire a mechanic to come along with you for the inspection. It could be money well spent.

If bringing someone along isn't an option, or you're worried that the particular boat is going to sell if you leave it too long to find a mechanic (a distinct possibility with certain used models in high demand), you're going to have to do the best you can, on your own.

For one thing, you should insist on a water test and go out there and try it. Does the motor start easily enough? Will it hold itself at idle? Any crazy smoke going on? How about small animals suddenly fleeing for their lives with their entire brood? Is it on fire, and are you now swimming? All of these are important questions to ask.

Once you get back in, and especially if the motor isn't running well, see if there are compression test results, or come prepared to conduct your own. Currently no task is beyond the scope of anyone with a smart phone willing to spend some data on a few online videos. Kits for testing this yourself are inexpensive. They come with a fitting attached to a gauge by a hose—nothing too complicated.

A compression test is a reading of how well an engine can compress the fuel and air in a cylinder. You figure this out by putting the fitting into the spark plug's threaded hole and then cranking the engine over through a few rotations while keeping an eye on the measurement reading on the gauge. Different motors have different desired ranges, and you can find these generally on the internet, the manual, or by calling the manufacturer. Regardless of the exact desired measurement, you'll want all cylinders to be within about 10% of each other. A compression test isn't necessarily an indicator that something will or won't go wrong in the future, but it can help you understand why the motor isn't running great now.

Other things to look for while checking the engine include how clean it looks (any mice nests?), how tight the fittings are on electrical components (any sign of corrosion?), and if the skeg and propeller both look like they're in good shape. A bent skeg and dented propeller not only can affect performance but can be indicators that there has been an unrepaired collision in the boat's lifetime.

As with the purchase of any large used item, service records are a definite plus, as would be purchasing the boat from the dealer that serviced it (or knowing who that dealer is if you're buying it from a private seller). Gremlins happen, and problems need to be troubleshot, which you'll pay for hourly. Wouldn't you rather take the boat to the same dealer who is familiar with its history and can quickly rule some issues out when something comes up?

You would never purchase a home without having it inspected, nor would you buy a used car without taking it for a test drive, so don't make the mistake of avoiding either when you're buying a used boat. It's going to be exceptionally frustrating to tow your boat a few hundred miles to the lake for the vacation your family has been dreaming of for months only to find that something doesn't work. Been there, done that, stomped on the t-shirt in disgust.

Buying a New Boat

Some people just aren't comfortable buying used. They'd rather be the first person to own the boat, so they are familiar with all its quirks and history. They figure this is worth taking the depreciation hit that comes along with buying new, and they might be right.

One nice thing about boats is that if you insure it properly, you'll only take the depreciation hit if you need to sell it suddenly. This is because most insurance companies offer an Agreed Amount Value policy. It is *exceptionally* important that you purchase this and **_NOT_** an

"Actual Cash Value" policy. It is so exceptionally important, that the "not" in the last sentence is the only word in this entire book that I've capitalized, underlined, bolded, *and* italicized. If I wasn't going for a black & white publication, it'd be in bright neon red as well. If you listen to nothing else, listen to this.

An Agreed Amount Value policy is a situation where you and your insurance company agree up front as to the value of your boat. In the case of a total loss, you will be paid that amount. Thus, you would want to ensure that the agreed value will cover what you owe on the boat. Then, if you are an accident and total the boat, you will not be stuck making payments on a vessel you no longer own or enjoy.

An Actual Cash Value policy (ACV in the acronym-rich insurance world) only provides coverage up to the current market value of the boat in the event of a total loss. In other words, depreciation is taken into consideration, so if you were hosed on the deal when you bought the boat and overpaid, and then immediately total it, you are not going to get back what you paid for it. You're going to get what it's worth. I trust you can see how this can quickly put you in a hole.

The stark difference in coverage comes with a stark difference in premium, with ACV policies being considerably less expensive than Agreed Amount Value ones. Even so, I would strongly urge that you purchase the more expensive Agreed Amount Value until you owe less on the boat than its actual market value.

There's a third type of policy that you should consider called Total Replacement Value. This takes the rising cost of new boats into consideration and will act to pay you the value of a new boat of the same make and model even if that cost has risen. For example, I was able to buy my boat new in 2013 for about $15,000 less than a new one would cost in 2016.

Before you get all excited, Total Replacement Value policies aren't good for the lifetime you own the boat. They typically have narrow coverage windows of a few years after which time they'll change to either an Agreed Value or Actual Cash Value policy. Even so, if you find a killer deal on a new boat, it might be worth considering one of these so that if you total it, you can get into another new boat which might not be as lowly priced.

I suppose the reason why such Total Replacement Value policies even exist these days is likely because boat prices have been skyrocketing lately. That's a bad thing when you're looking to buy a new one, but a good thing if you bought a desired make and model and need to sell it later. Higher new prices tend to mean higher used prices as well, so boats (especially from higher-end brands) tend to hold their value very well these days. It is not at all uncommon to see a decade-old boat commanding 60% or so of its original value. Just try that with the average used car and let me know how it goes.

Should you Finance the Boat?

Regardless of if you buy new or used, you may be in for some sticker shock. Not everyone can afford to pay the kind of cash it takes to buy these "toys," and so financing is very popular. As of 2019 at least, credit is available easily and for exceptionally long terms (10 to even 20 years) to keep monthly payments down. I would hope it would go without saying that if you sign up for a 20-year boat payment you're going to pay an insane amount of interest over the life of the loan. I certainly wouldn't recommend a deal that long, unless you intend to quickly pay the boat off.

There are some people who think you should never finance a toy and they might be right, but that depends on your financial situation as well as your place in life. The sad fact of the matter is that the prices have gone so high that it's difficult for most people to imagine owning all but the oldest and simplest of boats if paying cash. Faced with this, many choose to finance their purchase, and if your life is in order before you do so, there's no shame in it. Still, you need to *ensure* that your life is in order first.

I say the above because I'm concerned about your family and want to make sure you are alright. There are just too many people out there in debt to their eyeballs right now and I don't want you to hurt yourself by purchasing something that will almost certainly be a major expense. If you don't have a safe place for your kids to call home, food on the table, and a good emergency fund, hold off on the purchase.

If you do have those things, I wouldn't wait too long. "Tomorrow is promised to no one" and there's only so long that your kids are going to want to hang out with you. Soon enough they'll discover the opposite sex and become very embarrassed by you, so spend all the time with them that you can while they'll let you. If that means pulling the trigger and financing your boat, then so be it.

You'll find plenty of financial advisors who say I'm crazy. After all, taking the money that you would have spent on the boat and investing it instead will make your life better when you are 80 years old.

Big freaking whoop.

I love spending time with my children, and they want to spend time with me now. I'm not going to spend anywhere near as much time with them when I'm that old, and it's likely that neither will you. Now is your chance to make some memories and share some sunrises. Don't wait too long or you might miss your chance.

While I would never mortgage my kids' future for a boat today, I do have a minor, reasonable payment on a boat that is worth far more than I owe. I did pay a premium up front for a desired brand with good resale value and I do have confidence that, if ever needed, I could sell it very fast and escape the payment. When originally searching for it, I sought a holdover from the last model year and was able to negotiate a great price because of that. With new boat prices as high as they are these days, I consider the boat I'm making payments on an asset. I suppose it isn't so in the truest sense of the word as it has depreciated some and I won't make more on it than I paid, but it's something that I can convert to a good chunk of cash as needed if there were ever an emergency.

To me, financing a boat for a reasonable price so that I could spend time on the water with my kids made a lot of sense. I took my time with the purchase and made a thoughtful decision, so I feel I'll be fine financially later in life (or at least not doomed by the boat), but even if I wasn't, I have a feeling that a quick glance at a cherished photo from today will soothe me well enough.

10 – FISHING FROM A BOAT

So, you've bought the boat. Now what? It's certainly not as simple as driving it out to the middle of the lake and pulling fish in one by one. First, you need to get the boat safely to the lake, manage to launch it without embarrassing yourself too badly, and then take it to areas of the lake likely to concentrate fish. Once there, you're going to need to contend with wind, waves, and other boats and somehow position this hunk of aluminum or fiberglass in a fashion that might allow you to catch a fish or two, all without capsizing.

It can certainly be daunting, but we'll get you through it. You'll be on your way to making some great memories in no time.

Towing the Boat

To get your boat safely to the lake, make sure the trailer is properly attached to a vehicle that is rated to tow it. Different trailers have different locking mechanisms so look yours over or better yet have the person who sold it to you show how to connect it properly. Do a quick walk around with a spouse or buddy to make sure your lights are functioning and that nothing has been forgotten, and then off you go. While driving along, think back to all the times you've been behind a tractor trailer and saw the little sign that says, "vehicle makes wide turns." Remember that now, you're that guy. Forget it at your mailbox's peril.

Please don't be that person that is pulling a very large boat with a very small vehicle. You put your own life in danger and endanger others around you doing so. Owning a boat is expensive as it also means you need to own an appropriate tow vehicle. If you're towing something small like a johnboat, just about anything with a trailer hitch should do, but if your boat has any size or substance to it make sure you know its tow weight and then compare that to the tow rating of your vehicle. To be safe, don't exceed 80% of your vehicle's towing capacity, and remember that all the gas and gear in the boat adds up quick.

You'll find plenty of people on the internet advise you that their small little SUV or truck can pull a large boat and they're probably correct. That little SUV probably can *tow* the boat, but the better question is, can it *stop* that same large boat in time to avoid a collision? They likely don't have the experience of having tried, because if they did, they'd tell you to get a properly rated tow vehicle.

Backing a Trailer & Boat Ramp Etiquette

When you get to the lake, you're probably going to be nervous about backing your boat into the water. Take your time with the actual backing and be safe. Just make sure that you're ready to go once you've backed it in, and you aren't the guy trying to load the boat up while on the ramp – that will drive people crazy.

Your best bet is to try this the first few times on an uncrowded ramp. It's an excellent use of PTO to get away on a weekday when you might have some time to yourself. Watch a few videos on the internet until you're comfortable trying it yourself and then do as they do. Remember to use your mirrors and most important PUT IN YOUR PLUG! I have forgotten this twice and neither time was fun!

If you have a roller trailer, keep the boat firmly fastened until it's in the water. Do not disconnect the winch at the top of the ramp as your boat will launch there at the top of the ramp, kissing cement, ruining your day, and ticking off everyone waiting in line behind you.

Bunk trailers are bit less accident prone as your boat isn't going to slide from them easily unless there's some water to give it buoyancy, but I still like to keep mine connected to the winch until I'm close to the water. It's an extra step and probably unnecessary but I'm used to launching on some pretty steep ramps and I don't want to test the theory.

Launching a small boat by yourself isn't that hard if you invest in some strong dock line, and an even stronger hook. Tie one end of the dock line to the hook and attach the hook to the bow eye. Then, tie the other end of the dock line to the trailer, leaving 4-6' of slack. Back your boat in and you'll see it start to float. It won't go any further than 6', which will allow you to climb up onto the boat from the trailer and move it over to the courtesy dock. If there is no dock, use more slack so you can float the boat off the trailer and then pull it to shore.

When using this method, ensure that the hook you're using is strong enough to handle the weight of your boat. I once used one that wasn't and had a nice swim to retrieve my boat.

All of this gets easier with practice, and especially so without a ton of eyes on you. It can be easy to get flustered or embarrassed at a public launch if you don't do this much. Just remember that no one was born with this knowledge and everyone had to learn once too. We all remember this, and people will tend to be pretty understanding so long as you follow basic etiquette:

- Load up all your gear away from the actual launch – most places have a little area on the side where all the trucks will be lined up, ready to launch their rigs. This is the place that you want to put your rods into the boat, get your boots on, hook up your rope, etc. If you need more time, wave the guy behind you to go first. You do not want to do these things on the ramp itself.

- Turn off your vehicle headlights – they do nothing for you as you're backing your boat up and blind everyone in their path, especially if you're launching in low light conditions. If you're at a launch with numerous lanes, this can make things very difficult for others trying to launch at the same time.

- If possible, bring your spouse or friend along so they can control the boat while you park your vehicle. If this isn't possible, use common sense about where you tie your boat while you're parking. Try and leave it somewhere that it won't be in the way of the next guy. If there's a courtesy dock, tie to the side opposite of the launch, or at least as far back as you can. If there is no dock, beach your boat off to the side rather than right on the ramp. The idea is to get out of the way, so the next person doesn't need to wait for you to park and then get back to the water.

- The boat launch is not the place to hold a long conversation with friends, or, with your kids. If they're acting up, wait to deal with them after you're out of the way.

- If you need help, ask. We all get it, and no one is judging you half as badly as you think. Launching and retrieving a boat takes some getting used to. Doing it while keeping an eye on your kids is even more challenging. There is absolutely nothing wrong with admitting that you don't do this often and could use some help. We all want to get out there on the water safely and without incident. It does no one any good to stand idly by while you struggle, and you'll find that fishermen and women are very helpful folks in general, and even more so to help a respectful kid or their parents. I'd much rather help you for 5 minutes and be on my own way than watch you struggle for 50 and delay my own launch.

Once you get the boat launched and your kids safely on it, make sure you hook up to your kill switch as discussed in Chapter 3 and then get ready to have some fun!

The Seasons of Boating

There are a few predictable situations that you'll want to consider before you open the throttle. If it's early in the spring, the water tends to be higher which would usually mean you're less likely to bottom out, but the higher waters also mean that there's significantly more debris out there floating around. It doesn't take much of an object to knock a transducer off or damage a prop, so you want to be vigilant and take it slow. I've seen all sorts of debris out there from 8" blocks of wood to entire trees floating around. Obviously, hitting the latter would be a major issue, but even the former can do some damage (ask me how I know).

If you happen to spot something dangerous, mark it on your fish finder if you have one, or at least on a paper chart if possible. Granted, it's going to move slowly over time, but you'll usually find it in the same general area when you're on your way home, and this waypoint or dot will serve as a good reminder to be cautious as you approach the danger zone.

The risk of floating debris diminishes but doesn't disappear during the summer. The water levels are lower so there's less chance of various objects being carried off to sea from the shore, but on the other hand this also means that you now have a greater potential for running aground on a sandbar or other submerged hazard. A good navigational chart will help prevent this and you would do well to heed the various buoys out there on the water.

I've shaken my head more than once at folks who didn't know what these buoys were or how to navigate past them. You need to remember, "Red, Right, if Returning from the Sea." This means that you want to have a red buoy on your right or starboard side as you're returning "from the sea." A green buoy would be on your left or port side in the same situation. If you are heading towards the sea, the opposite applies.

For example, Lake Champlain runs north to south. The north is significantly wider and more "sea like" than the southern section, so when you're heading down south to Ticonderoga from Plattsburgh on the main lake, you generally want the red buoys on your boat's starboard side. In Crown Point, there is one point near buoy 34 where there is only a narrow section of water between the buoy and the shore. There's not a lot of room to maneuver, but it's extremely important that you stay in the channel, because there are four enormous cement pillars not far from the buoy and these sit in an exceptionally shallow flat and sand bar that is very hazardous to boats when the water level is low.

Sound carries well over the water and I've heard more than a few folks marvel at how "They really ought to put some sort of light on those pillars! Someone could be killed!" This is scary considering the buoy has a light on it and is literally right next to the pillars. The folks making this comment just had no idea what they were doing, so they cut through on the wrong side of the buoy and nearly wrecked. People like that share the water with you. Wear your kill switch.

Lakes tend to be packed during the summer as you get all the fishermen plus the pleasure boaters and jet skis. I wouldn't normally expect that the latter especially knows what they're doing, so keep a sharp lookout and don't trust those knuckleheads to abide by any rules, be it with buoys or even no wake zones. Weekend afternoons tend to be the busiest, as you could expect.

In the fall, the water levels tend to be even lower than they were during the summer, though this is a regional condition as some areas get a good amount of rain from tropical storms in August and September. Assuming you're in a temperate or drier zone, expect that any sandbar you scrapped by in summer is now more likely to ground you.

The good news about the fall is you'll probably have much of the lake to yourself as there are very few pleasure boats in the cooler water and many fishermen have turned their attention to hunting. The water is beautiful this time of year, especially in New England with its vibrant foliage. It's the perfect backdrop for a photo of your kid holding a massive northern pike or chunky smallmouth, and both species tend to be active this time of year.

You'll find even less folks out there in open water in the winter and frankly I wouldn't go out there that time of year with my kids. Float plan or not, if something goes wrong and you all wind up in the water, it doesn't take long for hypothermia to set in and you just can't count on someone seeing this happen and attempting a rescue. It's good to have other hobbies, anyway. Fishing and hockey complement each other very well in that when the water cools down too much, you can sharpen the skates.

The Wind and Waves – Driving in Rough Water

Mother Nature doesn't care what time of year it is or if it's your only week of vacation. She'll whip up a huge storm and monster swells just as easily in July as April. Be extra cautious about what seas you take your kids out in. Even if you can find a shallow bay protected from the wind, you'll still need to consider if you'll be able to get back home safe when you're done fishing. Use your best judgement. High seas compound every annoyance and make every peril more likely to occur. They are no place for your kids, and I keep a kite at the lake house for just this reason. If it's too windy to get them out on the water safely, take them out to a field and see how high you can get that kite flying. Trust me, kids love kites. It will save a day.

If you do go out there, or – more likely – those dastardly weathermen lead you wrong and you find yourself in trouble, keep things slow and steady and remain calm. Hopefully you're in a boat that has some business being out there in this weather (one of those multi-species or "walleye" boats discussed in Chapter 9 would do nicely), but don't let your boat give you a false sense of confidence.

High seas are a dangerous situation and you would do well to prepare yourself for these by reading as much as you can before you encounter them. Several boating and fishing forums have articles or threads on this topic written by people who have spent far more time on the ocean or Great Lakes than I ever will, so I highly encourage you to search around for them. I apologize if it seems like I'm ducking here, but I want to make sure that your family stays safe. www.boatus.com, www.walleyecentral.com, www.boatsafe.com are all great places to look for additional information, tips, and ideas. There are some great video demonstrations around the internet if you are more of a visual learner. Just search for things like "how to drive a boat in rough water," and you'll find more information.

Since you are here, I will, however, at least give you the basic theory of what you're trying to accomplish out there in heavy seas:

- Your goal is to get home safely, regardless of how much time it takes you. Forget those dinner reservations. You're going to be late. If you can hide and wait out the storm, that is your best option by far. If you get caught in a microburst or something particularly nasty, beach the boat if possible and get your kids on shore. Boats can be replaced. You can't replace your kid.

- The greatest danger of large waves is that they will force so much water into your boat that its balance and buoyancy are overwhelmed. This can happen from too much water coming over the bow when you spear the bottom of a larger wave because you're going too fast, or by a wave overtaking your stern because you are going too slow. Of course, a wave can also push water over your port or starboard gunnel because you're not moving at all and aren't facing into the wave.

- Because of the above, you don't want to approach waves head on. Rather, you want to hit the wave at about a 45 degree, or oblique, angle. This is a little counterintuitive because your boat is going to be rocking heavily as it slides up and down the wave, but this is what you need to do to keep as much water as possible in the lake and out of your boat. This will also tend to effectively double the amount of time it takes you to get back home because you'll find yourself driving a giant zig zag as you slowly make your way back. Better late than never!

- You need to actively drive, and that includes keeping a hand on the throttle. You want to manage your speed so that you aren't running into the backside of a large wave too quickly or allowing the waves behind you to hit you. Try to ride up and down each wave while taking care that you don't spear one.

- If you lose power and are caught in a storm, drop your anchor, a sea anchor (also known as a drift net), or bucket on a line off the bow to keep the bow facing into the waves. Let out as much line as you can and attempt to ride things out.

- Call or signal for help as appropriate if you find yourself overwhelmed. There's a reason the Coast Guard insists that you have several ways of signaling distress.

- Do bear in mind, of course, that if you get in trouble, another human being has to risk their own life to save you, so pay attention to the weather, make sure your boat is in good working order, and call it quits before things get too rough. Don't needlessly risk the lives of others. They are someone's kid or parent too.

- I certainly hope that it goes without saying that you will always want to be wearing your life jacket while under power, period, but certainly while being caught in weather such as this.

Being caught in a storm is a scary situation and not one that I would wish on anyone. I was caught in a microburst on Champlain once and it was not fun. The lake is sandwiched between the Adirondacks of New York and Green Mountains of Vermont and I wasn't paying enough attention to the weather reports. The storm was on me in what seemed like seconds with lightning and thunder crackling all around and the seas churning like crazy. I honestly thought I would be struck by lightning, capsize, or some combination of the two. God favored me that day, and so I was able to get to shore, beach the boat, and hop out. He even sent an angel along – the owner of that shoreline saw me and called out to me to come inside and wait out the storm. Events like that will reinforce your belief in a higher power and convince you that you finally need a smart phone so you can check the weather radar while you're out there!

Boat Control – Trolling Motors

Very high seas aren't the norm and most of us have the common sense to avoid them, especially when taking our kids out. With that said, perfectly calm water isn't normal either, so you're often going to find yourself dealing with wind. This can be a very good thing for fishing as the wind creates waves which reduce how much light can penetrate the water and really seem to turn on the bite for several species, but it does make boat control challenging.

The main reason that you want a boat in the first place is that it opens so many more places for you to fish. You really are limited when fishing from the bank, even more so with kids as they just can't get inside the tight corners that you can. Even so, that boat is useless if you can't keep it positioned where you want it as needed, so you're going to need to know some basics for boat control.

The best money I ever spent on my boat was purchasing a top tier trolling motor for it. I bought a trolling motor which has a bunch of great features, the best being the GPS anchoring system. The trolling motor has a little GPS sensor mounted inside and at the press of a button it will do its best to keep your boat in the same spot, regardless of the wind. As the wind picks up pace, so does the motor. As the wind calms down, the motor does too. It takes a little getting used to as you'll need to understand how much room it takes your motor to sort itself out, as the spot lock is not always instantaneous, but after you get a feel for it, it's quite reliable.

Some trolling motors come with a remote control which allows you to manage your boat control from anywhere, which is very useful when fishing with kids as you will spend a fair amount of time near them and away from the trolling motor. One word of caution is that if you accidentally hit a button on the remote, you could throw yourself out of the GPS anchoring system and not immediately notice it. This could be trouble if you're right near rocks or other hazards.

There are plenty of other fun things that you can do with these advanced trolling motors such as learning and then repeating your paths if you have a certain troll or drift that you'd like to try again. Some trolling motors even auto-deploy and trim themselves which can be handy if you're in the back helping your kids out and need to raise the motor depth as you head towards shallower waters.

Another great feature is that they have an automatic course heading, so that regardless of how the wind is blowing or the waves are crashing, your boat will maintain on autopilot in a constant heading. This is extremely useful and can work better than the GPS anchor at times for keeping you in one spot. I like to use this as I'm working windswept, rocky points for white perch with my son. I'll point the bow of the boat into the wind and press the autopilot. I'll then adjust my speed until the point where I'm holding steady into the wind. Sometimes, I'll go a bit faster so I can cover more of the point, and then reduce speed slightly or even turn off the motor so I can drift back. It's a nifty option!

Boat Control - Anchors

Fancy trolling motors aren't in the cards for everyone, so you may find yourself having to use the old standby – a trusty anchor. There's nothing wrong with that – it's all Grandpa ever had and worked well enough. I would suggest having two of them because depending on where you fish and what kind of wind direction you can expect to encounter, you might need to keep the boat situated in certain way to make sure all of your kids can cast out and fish prime water.

There are also items called sea or drift anchors that are basically a sturdy bag attached to a rope that you throw opposite of your drift. They won't stop you from moving completely but will slow your drift down enough that you can spend some time on a shoreline. If you don't have one of these, you can also make one with a large bucket and some rope. Once again, having two will help you position your boat better and in different angles.

If you're all-in with this whole fishing thing, they do sell a few different types of automatic shallow-water anchors. These are spikes that deploy downward from the stern of your boat and stick into the bottom, holding you in place. They can be pricy but on the other hand they let you sit exactly where you want to in shallow water, which can be a big deal if you're trying to keep your kids in range of some bluegill schools or beds on a windy day.

You'll notice that most professional bass fishermen have these on their boats, and a few walleye guys do too. One downside of a walleye-style boat is that it can be tough to fit two of these on and still have a boarding ladder, so you'll need to make do with one. This will be enough to hold you, but you might find yourself spinning from the wind. Just use some light power on your trolling motor to compensate for this, and you should be good to go.

Another downside of these tools is that they take up a lot of space on the back of the boat and are one more thing that needs to be cast around, so having only one might not be the worst thing in the world. Be mindful that they also take more vertical space, which could make it difficult to fit the boat into your garage. You can purchase a tilt bracket for some of the shallow water anchor models to alleviate this concern.

Boat Control – Working a Bank

One of the more productive ways to fish can simply be working your way down a stretch of coastline, weed line, or contour break that's holding fish. If there's a slight breeze you're usually better off just motoring up as far as you want to go into the wind and then drifting back down, working worms and lures as you go. You might need to make the occasional course adjustment with your trolling motor, but this can be relaxed fishing that affords a good amount of time for dealing with tangles. It is also a stealthy method, as the less time you're on your trolling motor, the less time a fish can hear it and panic.

As the wind picks up, this can be less effective as your drift will be too fast. This is when you want to use your trolling motor and troll into the wind. Attempting to move with the wind would move you too fast to fish and it would also be much more challenging to control the boat. Going into the wind will allow you more reaction time and control. If your trolling motor has some of the bells and whistles discussed above, all the better, but even without them, you just need an active foot to make this work. I would recommend doing this from a seated position unless you're confident with your sea legs.

Boat Control – Backtrolling

Backtrolling is when you put your main motor or kicker motor into reverse and drive the stern of your boat into the wind and waves. It's a good way to get wet if your boat isn't equipped with plastic splashguards, but it's also a great way to maintain precise control of your boat and slow down your approach, which is sometimes necessary if the bite is slow, or the fish are located in one condensed area.

Backtrolling is also very useful if you don't have a bow mount trolling motor, or if that trolling motor lacks any of the GPS anchor or autopilot features that I discussed above. You can achieve very similar effects with backtrolling, without having to spend a few extra grand on a fancy bow mount.

Boat Control – Beaching & Leaning

Sometimes it makes sense to let yourself get a little stuck. Granted you want to make sure you aren't going to damage your boat, and that you'll be able to get *unstuck* when necessary, but there's been plenty of times when I've let my boat gently float into the reeds or even a flooded tree so I could position my son for catching some fish. If you don't have a shallow water anchor, it can be the next best thing. Just be careful as this can damage your boat. If you're going to try this, raise your main motor up so it doesn't get damaged.

Obviously, certain objects can damage your boat while doing this, so if you are concerned about your paint job, you should avoid doing this. I am of the belief that a fishing boat is made to be used, so I am OK with a scratch here and there, but then again I tend to hold onto my larger purchases for many years – well past the point where a scratch is going to affect resale value very much if at all.

11 – THE LIFE OF A FISHING CHILD

Children grow up and their desires change. The same panfish that delighted your son when he was two probably won't do much for him as a snarky teenager, especially if he's been catching them consistently his entire life. Even so, it's vital to keep their interest in sports and hobbies when they become teenagers, because that is the age where they are exposed to the great dangers of drugs and alcohol. A kid who is looking forward to waking up at 5 a.m. to hit the water is not going to stay up all night getting drunk.

In this chapter we'll examine the different ages and phases that children go through when it comes to fishing so that you have your best chance of keeping them interested and safe. Every kid is going to be a little different but here are some general observations on the challenges they're going to face and how you can either introduce them to fishing at any given age, as not everyone will start in the same place.

Baby

As you've read here or on www.fishingfather.com, I started introducing my son to fish when he was only an infant. I have no idea if this made a difference or not, but he loves fishing now, so I assume it did. Infants kind of just stare at everything, but they have personalities and understand if you're excited about something. I'm pretty well-convinced that kids want to make their parents happy, so if you make a big deal out of fishing in front of an infant, their brain will start wiring to understand that this is important to the family, and they'll generally want to fit in.

Regardless, you are limited as to what you can do with an infant on a fishing trip. You're going to need another parent or grandparent to help with them. One adult needs to hold onto the child and the other needs to catch enough fish to keep showing off and entertaining them. Every time a fish is caught, make sure that you make a huge deal of it and bring them up to see it.

While it's generally frowned on to touch fish more than necessary, little wet hands aren't going to do much damage and the benefit of having another patron of the sport down the road outweighs any ill effect, so let them touch the fish (assuming it's not a "boo boo fish" of any kind) and get excited about doing so. My son has no problem holding fish while other kids are terrified of them. This could simply be personality, or it could be reflective of the fact that he's been exposed to them since he was only a few months old. I'm convinced it's the latter.

If your baby is old enough to clap, then that's a great way to get him or her involved in the show. They might not be able to cast, hook, or reel, but they can cheerlead. The whole idea at this stage is to get them excited about seeing fish pulled in, so that they'll want to do this themselves at their first opportunity. Clapping can't hurt.

Even if your baby doesn't take to fish immediately, positive exposure can help address any fears. My daughter started off a little scared of fish, but after seeing several dozen over the course of a week, she got used to them. If your kid is scared at first, obviously don't pressure them to touch the fish. Instead, make your big deal of them from several feet away. Forcing things would be disastrous.

Toddler

Once your kids grow into toddlers, they're going to want a rod of their own. They don't necessarily expect to catch any fish. In fact, I'm not certain that they even know how the fish wind up in the boat or on the shore just yet. All they know is that their mom or dad is casting a fishing rod and reeling it in, and they want to do this too so they can be just like their parents.

I was out with my son the other day and I saw another father with his daughter. She couldn't have been much more than 18-months. The father had his rod and the daughter was dragging around the bottom section of a two-piece rod. It didn't even have a reel, but that didn't seem to faze her at all. As far as she was concerned, she had her very own fishing rod and was out there with her daddy. I thought this guy had a great idea. Just give them something to hold onto—half a rod, a toy net, a bait bucket, whatever. Get them involved and give them a role to play.

Being someone who tends to go a bit overboard, I did have an entire rod, reel, and line setup for my little guy at that age. I just used an entry-level ice fishing rod as those are about the perfect size for a toddler. I took the hooks off a plug and would hand him the set up after casting it out and let him reel it back in. He was darn cute pretending to be just like me, and the photo was one for the ages (and the cover of this book).

Give your kid a toy rod to hold onto when you take them out for their first few fishing trips. All they want to do is reel in the line just like you.

As I've stated elsewhere, I was also helping him play with this fishing rod whenever we could, even inside our house. We had a very small colonial at the time with a living room that could seat all of two people comfortably, but that was all the space we needed to set him up for reeling in the line. I'd cast the plug into the corner, and he would reel it in. We'd do this as many times as he wanted, and sometimes mom or the dog would even play along by tugging on the plug and pretending to be a fish.

I also used to take him downstairs to look at my tackle. I have most of my stuff in those clear tackle boxes, which I didn't open because I didn't want him to stick himself with a hook. We would spend a lot of time peering at the crankbaits while asking each other, "Which one do you like?" as we looked through all the colorful lures. I'd get home from work and he would run up to me and ask me to go down in the basement to look at the lures.

When it was time for potty-training, it was done on the boat. We have a complete vinyl floor on our boat and figured we could always rinse it down if it came to that. Luckily, it never did. My son liked this just fine because as far as he was concerned, it was far better to stay out fishing and use the potty on the boat than come back to shore constantly for this new "chore."

Around the time he was being potty trained, my wife started teaching him how to cast out on his own, albeit only for short distances. She did this so I could continue concentrating on panfish for him to run up and reel in, to keep the action constant.

It didn't take him very long to learn, and eventually he and I would be able to truly fish together. We'd just hang out at the dock together, catching bluegills and sunfish that would hang out underneath. It was very difficult to get him to leave for lunch, so soon enough we just started packing it. We went through quite a bit of sunscreen in those days, and a few sun hats.

The Pre-School Years

My son entered pre-school just as his little sister was born, and I used some of my paternity leave to take him out fishing. My wife was so worn out from the whole birthing ordeal that she let me take him out all alone for the first time to a local lake. I had some trepidations as he was only three, but he handled it like a champ. I made sure to follow the advice I've laid out in this book, so we headed for some shady docks first to get the skunk out of the boat and a few sunfish in the livewell. Once that was done, I searched for some larger fish while he enjoyed his lunch and put him on a couple of bass.

That trip convinced me that he would be able to go out with me whenever the weather conditions allowed. No longer would we need to wait for his mother to wake up and join us, so we'd be able to get an early start and pick her up later. Everyone was happier.

By this age, he was able to cast quite well on his own most of the time, but not quite well enough to pick out the pockets in weed lines, or to avoid trees and other snags. Thus, he still relied on me for pinpoint casting, but if I put him in an area that held some panfish and was relatively open, he could catch plenty totally on his own.

Though I still tried to keep him away from all hooks, he became more adventurous at this age and started unhooking his fish and spearing worms on his own if I didn't get to them quickly enough. This meant it was time to start pinching those barbs.

Around the time that he turned four, I noticed he started to apply strategy to fishing. We would pull into a bay that looked a lot like one we had trolled in prior, and he'd suggest that we troll there as well. He'd also encourage me to take the boat deep into the reeds to try and find more nests of panfish.

I've read somewhere that we start holding onto memories starting at around three years old, so I'll be quite interested to talk to him years from now and see how much of all this he remembers. There were certainly some huge fish worth remembering!

This fish is one for any
four-year-old to remember!

The Grade School Years

Although there are pictures of Dad taking me fishing when I was just a toddler, I don't remember many fishing adventures until I was in First Grade or so. I spoke of one of these (in fact, the first of these) at the very beginning of this book and it remains a cherished memory.

I do know that I was able to cast quite well at six, and I'm fully confident that my son will be even better than me by then. I also recall being a voracious reader, favoring the In-Fishermen series on major freshwater game fish. I can vividly recall reading stories about the Mannheim Pike in the intro to their text on northern pike and being infatuated with the idea of one day traveling to Europe to tangle with a true monster.

I also recall being able to apply what I learned from those books. There were days when it was exceptionally windy and I'd relate how I had read that people had noticed largemouth were very neutral or inactive after being transported over bumpy roads in milk jogs, water sloshing to-and-fro. I suggested we find somewhere calmer, and once we moved, we started catching them.

Despite what you might think as they're clawing at their bedsheets, begging not to wake up for school, grade schoolers are very receptive to learning, especially if it's about something that interests them. If you can get them interested in fishing, you stand a very good chance of also getting them interested in reading. Thus, fishing can be a great way to increase their scholastic achievements.

Grade school is a long time where kids will develop substantially. Depending on the age and dexterity of your child, you might need to start them off with fishing tactics appropriate for toddlers, or you could move into more advanced concepts like you would with a middle schooler. For example, you probably wouldn't want to let a first grader take a fish off the hook, but a fifth grader would likely be fine in most instances (I'd still help them with the thrashing pickerel, but perhaps I'm being too cautious).

The Middle School Years

If you've been teaching your child to fish for several years, then by the time they hit middle school you should know if they enjoy it or not. If they don't, that's OK. It's not for everyone, but at least you tried, and they were able to make an informed decision. Your child will never be one of the poor kids in the world who laments that their parents never took them out fishing.

On the other hand, if you're just reading this now and your child is in middle school, you might only have a fleeting moment to capture their attention and spark their interest in fishing. Soon, they'll try to break off from the nest in every which way and could even become openly hostile to anything that's important to you. Middle schoolers can be awful!

At least they have an excuse. Middle school can be a very challenging time for kids. Many are going through puberty and having their first "relationships" with the opposite sex. In sports, it can be the first time where many kids are being exposed to the concept of try outs (although with the way things are going with this world and its "safe spaces," who knows if this will still hold true). It's a very awkward stage where teasing is rampant. I doubt anyone reading this book would say these were their best years of their life.

One way that middle school can be a little better is if your children are confident that they are good at something. They're unlikely to feel like such a loser if they understand that they can do something better than the bully. This won't necessarily convince the bully to leave your kids alone, but it will do wonders for how your children react to being bullied. When was the last time you heard about the fisherman caring that some degenerate idiot didn't like their hat?

Fishing is a much bigger deal now than it was when I was growing up. Both B.A.S.S. and FLW have tournaments for children in grade and middle school with scholarships and other prizes on the line. Nowadays, fishing is another travel sport and something your kids can draw some pride and self-esteem from.

If they're interested in pursuing fishing further, and making it one of their main sports, this would also be a good time to start reassessing your boat situation. Remember back in Chapter 9 when I told you that bass boats aren't that great for little kids, but come into their own as the youngsters grown and start getting interested in tournaments? Well, by middle school, you've arrived. You might want to start looking for a bass boat that can help them with this sport, if it's a main interest for them.

You don't want to break the bank, as you'll have expenses like college right around the corner but bear in mind that some schools are now offering fishing scholarships. If your kid is talented enough, a decently equipped bass boat could be a worthwhile expense. Some people spend thousands on sports camps over the years, which is fine, but consider that spending the same amount on a bass boat not only makes your child more competitive, but also allows you to go out with the rest of your family and continue making some great memories. It's worth considering once your kids are older.

The High School Years

It's never too late to develop an interest in fishing, but if your kids start in high school, they're probably going to teach themselves for the most part. There's nothing wrong with that, as it teaches independence and self-reliance. Teach them how to search the internet for articles and videos and watch the world open for them.

I would imagine, however, that it's pretty unlikely that they've managed to live in a fishing household for their entire life and only started participating in high school, so if you've jumped to this section, you're probably seeking a few tips for how you can help them out with their new love that is foreign to you.

I'd say that at this age the most important thing for them to remember is safety. High schoolers tend to think they're invincible, but I've yet to meet one who can breathe underwater or stop a moving propeller with their thigh. It would be a good idea to have them read the safety section of this book and quiz them on it a bit before cutting them loose.

The good news is that if they're truly just fishing, they shouldn't have any problem leaving you a float plan or checking in every now and then. All they're up to is good, clean fun, so what's the problem with calling mom or dad? Kids lie about where they *came from* at 5 a.m., not where they're *going*.

If you're lucky, your local high school might have its own bass fishing club or participate in the major sponsored events in the area. If neither is available, who is to say that you and your children couldn't be the first people to bring it to your region? It all must start with someone and pulling together something like that would make one heck of a resumé bolster (frankly, for you or your kid).

One thing that I would watch out for at this age is your kid getting carried away by the marketing that is pervasive in the fishing community. The entire sport is basically a giant advertisement with no shortage of people willing to tell you all the reasons you need to spend hundreds on every combo, or have a different rod rigged for every situation. If your kids aren't careful, they can end up spending a lot of money on this stuff chasing this gimmick or that. "The Bait Monkey" that convinces fishermen to part with their hard-earned dollars is a well-known devil in fishing.

Then again, remember that my core thesis for why you want your kids to fish in the first place is because if they're spending all their money on tackle, they don't have any left over for drugs! All I'm saying is that there is a balance to things, so keep an eye on them as they're very susceptible to marketing, and marketing is everywhere in fishing.

An astute parent might take advantage of that marketing situation and start kindling some ideas in their kid's head about how they might make a great living doing something they love after school is over. Being a successful, professional tournament fisherman (regardless of the species) is very hard to do, but that doesn't mean you can't have a great career in the fishing industry with a marketing degree. It's something for them to consider when they're exploring different colleges.

College and Beyond

Ok, so your kids are off in college. Congratulations, you have followed the advice in this book and elsewhere and raised efficient young anglers who are now off at school, probably near some lake, and fishing all on their own.

Perhaps they are members of the college fishing team, and they might have even earned a scholarship. They could be marketing majors, or perhaps even took an interest in the sciences because of fishing and are working on some degree in biology. You never know, maybe the cure for cancer is hidden in a panfish somewhere, and your kid will be the one to find it.

Because you have invested your time in helping your children learn this sport, you've helped raise a new generation of conservationists who will leave this planet a little better than they found it. You've taught them to think strategically, and to be life learners always seeking further knowledge. You've raised a person who will take a few moments to help others learn something difficult, and who won't lose their cool when things don't go exactly as planned. You've raised someone who, if the zombies ever do come, can feed and fend for themselves.

I hope that by this time, you have a lifetime full of memories with your family in the great outdoors, and that you were blessed with albums full of smiles, colorful fish, exotic vacations, and special moments.

I hope you can think back on a lifetime of boats just as though they were cherished pets and "remember that time" that your son caught his first pike from that old row boat, or when grandpa fell off the boat and into the water.

I hope you can remember that giant carp that broke off *just* as you were about to net it and finally laugh about it, or even better, get a hoot out of the time your daughter pierced your ear with a hook!

I hope you had countless mornings where you walked together with your kids down to the dock in awe as you watched the sun rise with all its glory, and countless evenings where you held them tight in a still bay while you watched it set.

In short, I hope that fishing with your kids was a life worth living.

ABOUT THE AUTHOR

John Paxton is the owner of www.fishingfather.com, a website dedicated to helping families learn to fish. He lives in New England with his wife and two children and spends as much time with them on the water as he can. He has been fishing across the United States from Alaska to Florida for over 30 years, with a considerable amount of that time spent fishing on Lake Champlain.

If you found this book helpful, please consider writing a review on Amazon as that will help others find and enjoy this book as well. You can also drop him a line at johnpaxton@fishingfather.com with suggestions for future books or articles that you would like to read on his website.

Made in the USA
Las Vegas, NV
06 June 2021

24294737R00105